DRESS
FOR SUCCESS

DRESS
FOR SUCCESS

Victor Maxwell

AMBASSADOR

BELFAST, NORTHERN IRELAND
GREENVILLE, USA

Dress for Success
© Copyright 2001 Victor Maxwell

ISBN 1 84030 096 5

Ambassador Publications
a division of
Ambassador Productions Ltd.
Providence House
Ardenlee Street,
Belfast,
BT6 8QJ
Northern Ireland
www.ambassador-productions.com

Emerald House
427 Wade Hampton Blvd.
Greenville
SC 29609, USA
www.emeraldhouse.com

Contents

Foreword

While a battle rages for the souls of men and women around the world, many Christians find themselves in their easy chairs content to watch the casualties of conflict. Yet, God bids all those who know and love Him not to be spectators but to engage in this intensive spiritual warfare. The outcome of the battle will ultimately affect the destiny of our family, our friends, our colleagues, and even our world. It is imperative to understand that this battle is not one that will be fought and won through the strong arm of the flesh, but rather by the might and power of the Spirit of God.

God has a strategic plan to win this age-old conflict. At the centre of that plan stands the Christian soldier. Believers are never described as creatures of comfort, and the church is not a showcase of saints. Rather, followers of Christ are frequently described in the Scriptures as soldiers. The key to any battle is the quality of the soldier. If the soldier is well trained and equipped properly, then he has a good chance of winning the war. However, with God our victory is not just a good chance. It is a certain triumph. The Bible says, "For the weapons of our warfare are not carnal, but mighty through God to the pulling down of strong holds; Casting down imaginations, and every high thing that exalteth itself against the knowledge of God, and bringing into captivity every thought to the obedience of Christ" (2 Corinthians 10:4, 5).

This spiritual battle is one of great intensity. We do not need to fear it. The safest place in the world to be is "in Christ." He is our hiding place. Paul, the great apostle, admonished us "to stand firm" in Christ. We do not need to be looking for demons under every bush. We only need to stand firm in Christ. We simply need to take our position in Him.

No good soldier would think of going into battle without being properly dressed and equipped to engage the enemy. We have defensive armour and offensive weapons. Our armour protects us, and our weapons enable us to "tear down Satan's strongholds."

Victor Maxwell provides sound Biblical teaching about the battle in which we are engaged and the armour of the soldier in this book. You will be challenged, inspired, and taught at the same time. Read with a heart of humility; a commitment to obedience; a love for the Saviour; and a passion to reach the world for Christ. You will come away with the knowledge of who you are; Who He is; and the battle to which you have been called. Awaken, oh soldier of God. The commander is calling. Get dressed. Put on the whole armour of God. The conflict is raging. The world is waiting. The devil is trembling. The victory is yours. You have been called into an eternal battle in which we are promised certain victory.

Sammy Tippit
International Evangelist

1

A Christian Soldier? Who Me?

Finally, my brethren, be strong in the Lord, and in the power of his might. (Ephesians 6:10)

The deacons met at the church on Monday evening to discuss necessary renovations to accommodate the growing congregation. One informed deacon proposed that the church should purchase a chandelier to improve the image of the sanctuary. Jake, the secretary of the church and a local farmer who resented city life, spoke up and said, "Brethren, what do we need a chandelier for? First of all, we don't have the money to buy it. Secondly, I can't spell it and furthermore, no one in the church can play it. What we really need around here is more light."

Just as there was confusion about a chandelier in the country church so also in Christendom there are a lot of fuzzy ideas of what a Christian really is. Some have the impression that a Christian is a person who is born in a Christian country and is given a Christian name. There is no such a thing as a "Christian country." Salvation is an individual matter. Therefore, a person is not a Christian by nationality. Others postulate that a person is considered to be a Christian because they were born in a Christian home. A Christian home is a great privilege, but we do not become Christians by the merits of our family. Each individual needs to be "born again." Some religious people sincerely profess to be Christian because they belong to a Christian church. A church does not have the power to save or regenerate anybody. We are not converted to Jesus Christ by the rite or ritual of a church no matter how orthodox that church may be.

If these commonly held views are not true, what is a true Christian? The Bible gives a very clear answer in definitive terms of what a Christian really is. Limiting our study to Paul's prison letter to the Ephesians, we find that throughout the epistle there are several telling cameos of what a true Christian is.

1. A Christian is a *saint* in the fellowship (Ephesians 1:1)

Three times in the first chapter of his letter to the Ephesians Paul refers to those who are "chosen in Christ" and "redeemed by the blood" of the Saviour as "saints" (Ephesians 1:1, 15,18). The designation "saint" suggests holiness or one who is set apart to be holy. It was an expression frequently used by Paul when referring to Christians in the first century. Sadly, the interpretation of this Christian appellation has been greatly distorted and has erroneously become the reserve of a designated few who have been canonized by the Roman Catholic Church on the grounds of each individual's merits. How foreign this interpretation is from the biblical meaning of what a saint is.

Consider the following contrasts:

A Saint according to tradition:	A Saint according to the Bible:
A person who died and is alive in eternity.	A person who is born again and alive on earth . (Ephesians1:1).

A Saint according to tradition:	A Saint according to the Bible:
A person who has been elected by the church.	A person who is chosen in Christ (Ephesians 1:4).
A good person who is recognised for their good works.	A saved sinner who is marred by their bad works. (Ephesians 2:1-4).
A person who has wrought a miracle.	A person who is a miracle. - Once dead and now alive in Christ (Ephesians 2:1).

Every Christian is a sinner saved by grace and set apart for God.

2. A Christian is a *citizen* of heaven and not a foreigner (Ephesians 2:11-19)

The Christian is in the world but not of the world. He is living here as a traveller with a passport for another land. Here in this world the Christian has no continuing city but is looking for one to come where he has an incorruptible inheritance which shall never fade away. The Bible describes the Christian as a pilgrim and a stranger in this world but not an alien to God. Although Christians are citizens of heaven and belong to the heavenly Jerusalem, they have responsibility on earth.

D. L. Moody, once met a man whose view on Christian citizenship was that a Christian should not participate in elections. When Mr. Moody asked the man if he was going to vote in the up-coming election he emphatically replied, "No, my citizenship is in heaven."

"Well, then," said Mr. Moody, "I advise you to bring your citizenship down to earth for the next ten days."

3. A Christian is a *stone* grounded on the Sure Foundation (Ephesians 2:20-22)

Paul further describes Christians by a metaphor which is

commonly employed elsewhere in the New Testament. He portrays the Church of Jesus Christ as the building of God. He emphasizes that Jesus Christ is the only foundation and the Christians are joined and "fitly framed together" as living stones for the function of a habitation of God by His Spirit. God commanded Solomon to build a glorious temple in which the Lord dwelt. God now builds a people in whom He is dwelling. Just as in a completed building every stone is cemented to the other so Christians are living stones which are vitally joined to each other.

4. A Christian is a *son* in the family of God. (Ephesians 3:6,15,18)

This is probably the best known and best loved of all the metaphors applied to Christians. It was this family relationship which prompted the Apostle John to exclaim, "Behold, what manner of love the Father hath bestowed upon us, that we should be called the sons of God" (1 John 3:1). Paul wrote that as Christians we are members of the household of God. (Ephesians 2:19) Being included in God's family means that we have been made fellow heirs with the saints (Ephesians 3:6) and we belong to the family of God (3:15).

5. A Christian is a *steward* who is required to be faithful (Ephesians 4:7-13)

A Christian is saved by grace and not by works, yet Paul told the Ephesians that as Christians they had received grace in the sense of a gift by which they were to serve God. All Christians are given gifts and as stewards of their gifts they are responsible for how they employ that gift in God's service. Our Lord told a parable of a varying number of talents which were given to different stewards. When the Master, the owner of the talents, went to a far country, the stewards received the instruction, "Occupy until I come." In the same sense Christians today are to put the gifts God has given them to the very best use for our Lord and Master. As Christians we will all appear before the Judgment Seat of Christ to give an account of the deeds we have done. Will we hear, "Well done thou good and faithful servant?"

6. A Christian is a *student* who follows his Master (Ephesians 5:1)

The word that is consistently used for a follower of Jesus Christ in the New Testament is a disciple, which is a student or an imitator of the Lord Jesus Christ. The greatest mark and distinction of belonging to Jesus Christ is a likeness to Him. Murray McCheyne of Dundee prayed, "Make me as holy as it is possible for a saved sinner to be." True holiness is likeness to Jesus and that likeness is encouraged in chapter five of Ephesians by walking in the love of Christ and in the light with Christ.

7. A Christian is a *soldier* in the fight of faith (Ephesians 6:10-20)

Paul's letter to the Ephesians is the first of his pastoral epistles, letters written while Paul was a prisoner in Rome. Philippians, Colossians and Philemon were also written while the apostle was incarcerated. Being in Rome was a new experience for Paul and especially the close attention given to him by the Imperial Roman soldiers who guarded him day and night. These soldiers, dressed in full armour, gave Paul the first hand insight he needed to see the role of the Christian in conflict.

The New Testament is replete with references to Christians as combatants at war. This militant aspect of the Christian experience has become unpopular with many Christians in recent times. Many prefer to think that the Christian life is a playground with user-friendly toys rather than a battlefield with real weaponry. In this study we will focus on this final aspect of the Christian as a soldier.

Ephesians is a letter that begins with the Christian sitting (2:6); it progresses with the disciple walking (5:2) and ends in chapter six as a rallying call for all Christians to stand (6:11).

Note this outline of Ephesians:

Chapters 1-3   The Christian's wealth in Christ -
                He is sitting in Christ

Sadly we live in a time when there is little sense of Christian conflict. There are some who want to remove all the hymns with military themes from our song books. They tell us that hymns such as "Onward Christian Soldiers," "Hold the Fort for I am Coming" and "Who is on the Lord's side?" are too militant. Yet one cannot read the New Testament and fail to sense the clear call to spiritual warfare.

Consider the following verses:

"And I say also unto thee, That thou art Peter, and upon this rock I will build my church; and the gates of hell shall not prevail against it" (Matthew 16:18).

"For the weapons of our warfare are not carnal, but mighty through God to the pulling down of strong holds; Casting down imaginations, and every high thing that exalteth itself against the knowledge of God, and bringing into captivity every thought to the obedience of Christ" (2 Corinthians 10:4-5).

"This charge I commit unto thee, son Timothy, according to the prophecies which went before on thee, that thou by them mightest war a good warfare; Holding faith, and a good conscience; which some having put away concerning faith have made shipwreck" (1 Timothy1:18-19).

"Fight the good fight of faith, lay hold on eternal life, whereunto thou art also called, and hast professed a good profession before many witnesses" (1 Timothy 6:12).

"Thou therefore, my son, be strong in the grace that is in Christ Jesus. And the things that thou hast heard of me among many witnesses, the same commit thou to faithful men, who shall be able to teach others also. Thou therefore endure hardness, as a good soldier of Jesus Christ" (2 Timothy 2:1-3).

"For I am now ready to be offered, and the time of my departure is at hand. I have fought a good fight, I have finished my course" (2 Timothy 4:6,7).

Repeatedly in the scriptures the Christian life is seen in terms of warfare. Living for Jesus Christ has always been a conflict, and it will never cease to be. Whether you are at the beginning of your Christian experience or mature in your Christian walk, the conflict remains. Furthermore, I find the more effective a Christian becomes the harder Satan will work against him. However, it is also true that the longer we fight and the more victories we gain the more our faith will be strengthened.

Ephesians 6:10-18 is a perfect conclusion to all Paul has written in this letter. If we are true Christians as defined in the earlier chapters and are living the way a true Christian should live, then we can be sure of one thing...we are going to run into the enemy. It is impossible to live in the manner that Paul outlined to the Ephesian Christians without having opposition from Satan. It is this conflict that prompted Paul to conclude with the exhortation, "Finally, my brethren, be strong in the Lord, and in the power of his might. Put on the whole armour of God, that ye may be able to stand against the wiles of the devil."

On April 18, 1775, Paul Revere set out on his now famous midnight ride. His journey took him to the house of John Clarke who was the Pastor of the first Parish Church in Lexington, Massachusetts. Revere's reason for stopping at this house was to warn Samuel Adams and John Hancock, leaders in the American Revolution, that the British had issued warrants for their arrest. Consequently the decision was made in the church parsonage to call up the minutemen to face the British.

The first shot of the American Revolutionary War was fired on the church green of John Clarke's church. In this the first battle of the Revolutionary War, eight Americans were killed. Ten more Americans and one British soldier were wounded. By the time news spread to Concord that the British regulars were firing on Americans, many more minutemen joined up for the conflict that ultimately resulted in the defeat of the British forces and American independence. On a memorial stone on the green of the Parish church in Lexington these words of Captain Parker are chiselled into granite, "Stand your ground. Don't fire unless fired upon but if they mean to have a war let it begin here."

Christian, our war has already begun. Stand strong on your grounding in Christ. Reflect on the words of Maltbie D. Babcock, "We are not here to play, to dream or to drift. We have hard work to do and loads to lift. Shun not the struggle. Face it." Victories are never won while resting in the barracks. Christ's soldiers must always be alert, armed and able for the war.

C. T. Studd, the famous and rich English cricketer who forsook his fortune to serve as a missionary in China, India and eventually Africa where he died, wrote many quaint poems which were published in the magazine of the Worldwide Evangelization Crusade of which he was the founder. One such poem published in November 1925, reflects something of his parallel thoughts of the Christian soldier and the European Crusaders whole tried to recapture the Holy Land in the Twelfth Century.

The Crusaders of old were a funny crew,
But I love them with all my soul,
For they left their all and risked their lives,
And fought to achieve their goal.

Now who will be a Crusader bold,
Of the twentieth century,
To evangelize the whole wide world ?
'Tis the will of the Trinity.

The Crusaders of old wore great long swords,
And were clad in armour bright
Crusaders today wield the Book of God
Their armour " The Lord of Light."

Crusaders of old wore a visible cross,
Which the blind could almost see
Crusaders today preach the Word of the Cross
The Gospel of liberty.

Crusaders of old travelled very far,
To the land of the Saviour's birth;
Crusaders today go farther still,
To the uttermost parts of the earth.

Of old a man wasn't reckoned a man
By a worthy Christian maid,
If he hadn't forsaken home and all
And fought in a great Crusade.

You need not be extremely wise
With grammar spick and span,
To go and teach the love of God
In the darkest haunts of man.

You need not be of royal birth,
Or a demi-millionaire,
To go and cut the bonds of slave:
Who lie bound in the devil's lair.

You need not wear peculiar clothes,
Nor possess a swagger degree,
To publish abroad why the Son of God
Died on Calvary.

But you need to have a simple faith
And a love for God and man,
A heart which laughs at risks and fears,
And be a humble man.

But mind, hit hard! play the game! don't fear!
Tho' the pitch be badly queered:
For God needs "Drakes," not dear little ducks,
To singe the devil's beard.

Now I will join the Crusader band
Of the twentieth century

To teach the lost the love of God,
Revealed on Calvary.

So write my name upon the roll
A soldier of Elohim
How can I face my God unless
I've lived and died for Him?

STUDY QUESTIONS

1. What is the Biblical definition of a true saint?

2. How does one become a citizen of heaven?

3. Since all Christians are members of one body how should they relate to each other?

4. If the Christian life is an "imitation of Christ" what should the dominant features of our lives be?

5. What features of your Christian life give evidence that you are in a spiritual conflict?

2

Your Posture is Important

Put on the whole armour of God, that ye may be able to stand against the wiles of the devil. (Ephesians 6:11)

Dudley Tyng was a young uncompromising Episcopalian preacher in Philadelphia during the great spiritual awakening in the middle of the nineteenth century. Periodically he organised noonday meetings at the YMCA in downtown Philadelphia at which great crowds came to hear the dynamic young preacher. At the meeting on Tuesday, March 30, 1858, over five thousand men gathered to hear Tyng preach from the text, "Ye that are men, go and serve the Lord" (Exodus 10:11). Over one thousand men committed their lives to Jesus Christ.

During the course of his sermon the young preacher exclaimed, "I must tell my Master's errand, and I would rather that this right arm were amputated at the trunk than that I should come short of my duty to you in delivering God's message." A week after this event Dudley Tyng visited the Pennsylvanian countryside and watched men work at a corn threshing machine in a barn. Accidentally the young preacher caught his loose sleeve between the cogs of the machine. His arm was severely lacerated. The main artery was severed and the median nerve was severely damaged. As a result of the severe injuries and shock Dudley Tyng died.

A group of sorrowing friends and ministers gathered at Tyng's deathbed and one of them asked him for a final statement. Mr. Tyng feebly whispered, "Let us all stand up for Jesus."

On the Sunday following Rev. Dudley Tyng's death his close friend and fellow worker, the Rev. George Duffield, pastor of Temple Presbyterian Church in Philadelphia, preached the morning sermon as a tribute to his ministerial colleague. He concluded his sermon by reading a poem that he had just written in tribute to the final words of his great friend.

Stand up, stand up for Jesus; ye soldiers of the cross;
Lift high His royal banner-it must not suffer loss.
From victory unto victory His army shall He lead,
'Till every foe is vanquished and Christ is Lord indeed.

Stand up, stand up for Jesus; the trumpet call obey;
Forth to the mighty conflict in this His glorious day.
Ye that are men now serve Him against unnumbered foes;
Let courage rise with danger and strength to strength oppose.

Stand up, stand up for Jesus; the strife will not be long;
This day the noise of battle-the next, the victor's song.
To Him that overcometh a crown of life shall be;
He with the King of Glory shall reign eternally.

Paul exhorted the Christians in Ephesus to walk as saints in the pagan world and to stand as soldiers for the Saviour. Standing for God means to not quit. It hints at a "no surrender attitude" which demands confidence and courage in spite of prevailing circumstances.

I am reminded of the almost life-size doll which kids punch and although the doll falls over it immediately springs back upright again. The doll just will not lie down. Likewise Christians need to be those who refuse to lie down. They must bounce back up again when Satan tries to trip them.

During the Battle of Waterloo when the fight was grim and hard, an officer galloped up to the Duke of Wellington and reported on behalf of his superior officer that they were being destroyed and could not hold the position unless reinforcements arrived soon.

The "Iron Duke" said to the soldier, "Tell him to stand."

The soldier rushed back and delivered the message to his senior officer. Within moments another officer came with the same request for reinforcements. The Duke's answer was the same again, "Tell him to stand."

That soldier returned to the battle front and a third soldier came begging in the name of his superior officer for the needed help. "I have no help to send you," said the Duke, "Tell him to stand."

The soldier saluted and said, "You will find us there, Sir." When the battle was fought and finally won, the Duke found them, all of them, dead in their place. They were prepared to stand and to die in their place for the "Iron Duke."

Merchant seamen from all over the world disembarked at the magnificent harbour on the Cayster River in Ephesus. They not only brought their cargoes of gold, silver, ivory and precious stones to add to the luxuriant life-style of the Ephesians, but they also came to indulge and contribute to the moral pollution and decadent corruption of the great city which was generally known as the "market of Asia." Superstition and witchcraft, practised by both Jews and Greeks, abounded among the people. The majority of the Ephesians venerated the greatness of the Greek god Jupiter and "Diana of the Ephesians."

Paul became acquainted with Ephesus while he and his missionary friends spent two years preaching and teaching God's Word in that city. From his personal experience in Ephesus Paul knew that it would not be easy for Christians to be followers of Jesus Christ in such a promiscuous and superstitious atmosphere. Indeed, to enable them to walk with Christ they needed to know how to stand without wavering for Jesus Christ in the face of spiritual darkness and moral decadence.

To enable a Christian to stand for the truth in Ephesus or in any society Paul wrote of the provision and protection the Lord has made for all Christian soldiers.

1. The enlistment of the Christian soldier (Ephesians 6:10)

"Finally, my brethren, be strong in the Lord, and in the power of his might." When Paul addressed his "brethren" he was not speaking to a group of spiritual elite, he was addressing *all* believers in the Ephesian church. Likewise, *all* Christians are expected to put on *all* of the armour and are to be ready at *all* times to stand for Jesus Christ.

Timothy was serving God in Ephesus when Paul wrote to him on the same subject, "Thou therefore endure hardness, as a good soldier of Jesus Christ. No man that warreth entangleth himself with the affairs of this life; that he may please him who hath chosen him to be a soldier" (2 Timothy 2:3,4)

As Christians we dare not try to cherry pick which role we wish to fulfill. Some may be content to be looked upon as saints or even the children of God, but we cannot escape the fact that God has also chosen all His saints and sons to be soldiers.

He did not command the Christian to be a five star general or to have any fancy band parades. An American Chief of Staff spoke somewhat disparagingly of the British Army, "It just makes you want to cry; they are no longer a great power. All they've got left are generals and admirals and bands." Let not that be said of Christianity. The Lord is the Captain of our Salvation and has enlisted us to be His soldiers.

Paul lists two distinguishing features that are required of a Christian soldier. First, the soldier of Jesus Christ should learn to endure hardness. Every soldier must learn to accept the discipline of army life in order to prepare himself for battle. The second feature is that the Christian recruit should have one primary aim, to please his Captain. The believer must devote himself exclusively to his work as a soldier in order to receive his Commander's commendation.

In the light of such discipline and devotion to Jesus Christ how many true soldiers are there in Christ's army?

2. The encouragement for the Christian soldier to be strong (Ephesians 6:10)

"Finally, my brethren, be strong in the Lord, and in the power of his might…" "In Christ" is one of the key clauses in Paul's letter to the Ephesian Christians. Although they lived in Ephesus they were secure "in Christ." This little clause not only provided a sense of security as to their spiritual position and protection but also indicated the sufficiency they enjoyed in Christ.

Our sufficiency and strength to stand for Jesus Christ wherever God has placed us is only in the Lord. The Psalmist affirmed, "The Lord is my strength and song, and is become my salvation" (Psalm 118:14). It would have been perfectly orthodox to declare, "The Lord is strong…" or even more emphatically, "The Lord is almighty." However, he had proved God's strength personally in national calamity and physical infirmity and therefore could say, "The Lord is *my* strength …"(italics mine). It should also be noted that he did not say, "The Lord *was* my strength…" as though he boasted of a past experience. He was up to date in proving that God's strength is sufficient for every day.

Paul not only exhorted that we should be strong in the Lord, but he proceeded to outline the formidable enemy all Christians face and then described the armour that will enable us to face this fierce foe. Closer examination of the Christian's armour will show that this is nothing less than being clothed with Jesus Christ Himself. We can only be strong when we are dressed with Christ.

3. The engagement of the Satanic foe (Ephesians 6:11,12)

"Put on the whole armour of God, that ye may be able to stand against the wiles of the devil. For we wrestle not against flesh and blood, but against principalities, against powers, against the rulers of the darkness of this world, against spiritual wickedness in high places." Six times in these two verses the word "against" is repeated. Every Christian knows that he is up against the powers of evil. Satan, sin and hell are against the believer. Furthermore, every Christian should have a declaration of war against the Devil.

The Christian is not only engaged in a titanic battle. He is up against Satanic and supernatural powers. It is important for us to be aware that behind all sin, its foul action and filthy stains, there is a real and supernatural Devil. It is against him and his emissaries that we are wrestling. Let us remember that Satan is supernaturally strong, skilfully subtle and seriously sinister. He is the Christian's arch enemy.

- James tells us to "Resist the devil, and he will flee from you" (James 4:7).

- Peter warned Christians in the troubled times of the first century, "Be sober, be vigilant; because your adversary the devil, as a roaring lion, walketh about, seeking whom he may devour: Whom resist stedfast in the faith, knowing that the same afflictions are accomplished in your brethren that are in the world" (1 Peter 5:8,9).

- Paul admonished Christians of his time to be vigilant "Lest Satan should get an advantage of us: for we are not ignorant of his devices" (2 Corinthians 2:11).

- Paul also warned the Ephesians of an impending attack on their church, "For I know this, that after my departing shall grievous wolves enter in among you, not sparing the flock. Also of your own selves shall men arise, speaking perverse things, to draw away disciples after them. Therefore watch..." (Acts 20:29-31).

Charles Wesley knew much about conflict in his Christian life. Many times both he and his brother John were physically abused for their evangelical stand. They published a hymn in 1749 which was titled *The Whole Armour of God-Ephesians VI*. The hymn which is a strong call to arms has often been referred to as the Christian's bugle blast.

Soldiers of Christ, arise,
And put your armour on,
Strong in the strength which God supplies
Through His eternal Son:

Strong in the Lord of hosts,
And in His mighty power;
Who in the strength of Jesus trusts
Is more than conqueror.

Stand then in His great might,
With all His strength endued;
And take, to arm you for the fight,
The panoply of God.

From strength to strength go on;
Wrestle and fight and pray;
Tread all the powers of darkness down
And win the well-fought day.

4. The equipment for the Christian's strife (Ephesians 6:13-20)

"Wherefore take unto you the whole armour of God, that ye may be able to withstand in the evil day, and having done all, to stand. Stand therefore, having your loins girt about with truth, and having on the breastplate of righteousness; And your feet shod with the preparation of the gospel of peace; Above all, taking the shield of faith, wherewith ye shall be able to quench all the fiery darts of the wicked. And take the helmet of salvation, and the Sword of the Spirit, which is the Word of God:" (Ephesians 6:13-17)

Just as a nation equips its soldiers for war so God has provided Christians with all that they need to wear in this spiritual war. It is not sufficient to wear some of the armour. All of the armour is needed if we are going to be able to stand for Christ and withstand the evil one. Furthermore, the Christian armour was made to measure and no armour was provided for the soldier's back as no provision was made for retreat. The Lord has provided for every eventuality for the victorious Christian life and no area of the Christian's life is left unprotected.

When David volunteered to face Goliath, King Saul tried to fit out David in armour that was not made for him and did not belong to him. The ill-fitting armour was of no use to David so he discarded it and went to meet Goliath in the strength of the Lord.

5. The endurance of the Christian's service (Ephesians 6:18)

"Praying always with all prayer and supplication in the Spirit, and watching thereunto with all perseverance and supplication for all saints." To stand for Jesus Christ and withstand the evil one perseverance is necessary. Perseverance is stickability, enduring hardness, keeping on until the race is finished and the battle is won.

The Lord gave instructions to the people of Israel as they marched through the wilderness en route to the Promised Land, "And the officers shall speak further unto the people, and they shall say, What man is there that is fearful and fainthearted? let him go and return unto his house, lest his brethren's heart faint {Hebrew - melt} as well as his heart" (Deuteronomy 20:8). This reminds us that the battle is not for the faint nor fearful. Victory is for those who persevere.

Sir Winston Churchill was undoubtedly the greatest war leader of the last century. On October 29, 1941, when German planes were raining down their bombs every night on London, he was invited to give an address at Harrow School where he had formerly been a student. From the lectern he looked defiantly at the student body and gave a speech that no one present ever forgot. The sum total of that speech was, "Never give in. Never give in. Never. Never. Never. Never. In nothing, great or small, large or petty, never give in except to convictions of honour and good sense. Never give in." Churchill then sat down. Britain, Europe and the Western world was freed from Nazism because Churchill never gave in.

The Christian need never give in or give up.

6. The enjoyment of the Saviour's victory (Ephesians 6:10,13)

No provision was made for defeat for the Roman Legionnaire. The Emperor expected only victory, nothing else. As Christians we are not fighting for victory. We are moving in victory. In Paul's admonitions no mention is made of gaining ground. Victorious

Christians are standing on the ground that Jesus has already conquered for us.

In 1983 a television journalist interviewed a British army general during the Falklands conflict in which Britain was at war with Argentina. The journalist posed this question to the general, "Will you win this war?"

To this the military man replied sharply and without hesitation, "There is no doubt about it. We will win this war."

The journalist was somewhat taken aback with the strident confidence of the general and further pressed with another question, "Why are you so sure that you will win the war?"

The British general explained, "There is no doubt that we will win because of four reasons:

The rightness of our cause – it is just. Argentina is the aggressor;

The superiority of our weapons;

The commitment of our soldiers. We are better trained and better disciplined.

The demoralization of our enemy."

Enough was said. The battle was won. The parallels to Christian warfare are obvious.

STUDY QUESTIONS

1. Why is it hard to withstand the Devil as a Christian?

2. Write a list of some areas where you need to stand for Jesus Christ.

3. Christians can be discouraged. Identify four main areas of discouragement in your life and indicate how these can be overcome.

4. When should the Christian dress up for conflict?

5. Reread the answer of the British general about the Falklands War and identify parallels in the Christian's spiritual conflict.

3

Hand Picked

Wherefore take unto you the whole armour of God, that ye may be able to withstand in the evil day, and having done all, to stand.
(Ephesians 6:13)

On a pastoral call I entered a dimly lit house to visit a sick gentleman. "Well, how are you today Billy?" I asked him.

"I'm run down Pastor." he replied as he struggled to sit upright.

The term "run down" has nothing to do with a traffic accident or athletics. It is the expression we commonly use when we are be low par and attribute it as the underlying cause of so many of our physical ailments. To be run down generally means we are at a low ebb physically. Sometimes this physical draining is manifested in exhaustion or an eruption of boils or abscesses in the body.

Boils and abscesses are tell-tale evidences of a war that is being carried on internally. In our blood stream red and white corpuscles flow side by side. They are like a great army. The red corpuscles are the regular troops which carry supplies of oxygen and nutrients to all parts of our body. The white cells are the infantry who fight against infection.

Often we become "run down" when our bodies are under attack by some bacteria and the white cells fail to do their job adequately. When this battle rages within your body and the white cells mobilise to quench the foreign germs, many cells, germs and some body tissues, die. The eruption of boils are only graveyards on the battle field of your body that indicate the infantry soldiers in your blood stream are coping with their job.

As there is a continual war taking place in the physical body, there is also a constant battle going on within the spiritual realm. The first mention of the word "church" in the New Testament implies that the church of Jesus Christ is under attack. "And I say also unto thee, That thou art Peter, and upon this rock I will build my church; and the gates of hell shall not prevail against it" (Matthew 16:18).

Sadly, there are many Christians who are unaware of this constant conflict and furthermore they refuse to become involved. Just as the white cells of the "run down" body sometimes fail to do their job, so also in the "run down" church there are many Christians who fail to play their part.

When the apostle Paul penned the words, "Finally, my brethren, be strong in the Lord..." (Ephesians 6:10) he was not writing the "finally" of a concluding theme.   Rather, he was writing it as the commencement of the climax to his letter. Like the pointed finger of the military figure in the familiar wartime poster with the caption "Your country needs you," so Paul calls for all Christians to take their stand on the Lord's side.

Spiritual conflict was not a new phenomenon limited to Paul's day. The history of God's covenant people, Israel, is constantly punctuated by the conflicts they faced. When Moses led the people of Israel out of Egypt and toward the Red Sea they were pursued by the armies of Pharaoh. As God's people left Egypt they were a race of liberated slaves who immediately became enlisted in the Lord's army. Hence the Lord declared, "The LORD is a man of war: the Lord is his name" (Exodus15:3). It was then that Moses challenged the people and asked "Who is on the Lord's side? let him come unto me. And all the sons of Levi gathered themselves together unto him...thy servants will pass over, every man armed for war, before the Lord to battle, as my lord saith" (Ex. 32:26; Num.32:27)

The spiritual conflict is the war of the ages. Since the fall of Lucifer there has always been the struggle between light and darkness, between heaven and hell, between truth and error, between the Prince of Life and the ruler of darkness. We know that all who are in Christ are on the winning side even though the Devil is a defeated foe. He is like a trapped animal and still rages against the Lord's people today. As Christians we are to be aware that we are in a battle.

Paul reminded the Ephesian Christians that they were not in a physical nor visible battle. Instead it is an occult war. It is the invisible battle of the mind where the raging Devil seeks to reek havoc on the people of God by infiltrating and corrupting their minds. It is the hidden battle of the home where the Devil is having a heyday with the breakdown of many marriages and rebellion against authority. Marriage is in crisis and parental control is almost a losing battle. We face an increasing battle for the youth of our land and the children in our schools. It is the subtle battle of ecumenicity which is seeking to foist upon Christendom a false church which preaches a false gospel. As Christians we need to stand up for Jesus against these diabolical currents from hell which are designed to destroy us.

As Christian soldiers who have heard the call to arms in spiritual warfare, we dare not be ignorant of the Devil's devices. Christians cannot afford to be indifferent and not involved in the conflict. Today there is a clarion call to arms for all Christians.

When Paul likened the Christian to a soldier prepared for war it is important to note that imperial soldiers and military garrisons were familiar landmarks in the Roman and Greek world of the first century. Therefore it was not strange to Christians of that time that Paul should consistently draw parallels to Christians such as Archippus and Epaphraditus as soldiers of King Jesus (Philemon 2, Philippians 2:25).

Paul's call to war was prefaced by the inclusion of all Ephesian Christians; "Finally, my brethren..." This suggests to us:

1. The recruitment of the Christian soldier

Paul addressed every member of the Christian Church as a soldier of Jesus Christ. Paul's words were not directed exclusively to pastors at Ephesus but to all believers. As Christians we are expected to be clad in the whole armour of God at all times.

The Christian soldier must be a citizen. It makes sense that in order to be a soldier of a nation a person must be a citizen of that country. There must be loyalty to the king and the kingdom. Paul already reminded the Ephesian believers that they were no more strangers, but due to their salvation in Christ they were fellowcitizens of the heavenly Kingdom.

Moses commanded the children of Israel, "Take ye the sum of all the congregation of the children of Israel, after their families, by the house of their fathers, with the number of their names, every male by their polls; From twenty years old and upward, all that are able to go forth to war in Israel: thou and Aaron shall number them by their armies" (Numbers1:2,3). Every male slave delivered out of the kingdom of Pharaoh was enlisted as a recruit in the army of Jehovah.

The Christian soldier is chosen and commissioned. "No man that warreth entangleth himself with the affairs of this life; that he may please him who hath chosen him to be a soldier" (2 Timothy 2:4). What a high honour it is to be enrolled among God's soldiers.

Paul also posed the question, "Who goeth a warfare any time at his own charges?" (1 Corinthians 9:7). None of us has chosen this battle. We are chosen by God for the conflict. It is an encouragement to know that all of God's soldiers are hand picked, called by their name and allocated to their division and location in God's army.

The Christian soldier must be constantly available. King Solomon gave the following directive to his armed forces, "And there is no discharge in that war" (Ecclesiastes 8:8). Involvement in this battle of the ages has nothing to do with how long we have been on the Christian pathway. From the moment of our conversion until we are called up to heaven from the conflict or caught up by the coming of the heavenly King, there will be no discharge from this fight.

2. The requirement of the Christian soldier.

The Christian soldier must be strong in the Lord. "Finally, my brethren, be strong in the Lord, and in the power of his might"(Ephesians 6:10). In Paul's epistle to the Ephesians he majored on the "riches" that the believer has in Christ. As sinners redeemed by Jesus Christ we have substituted our poverty for His wealth. Likewise we are to exchange our weakness for His strength. Dr. F. B. Meyer wrote, "Many would be strong, but fail because they forget that they can be effectively so only 'in the Lord and in the strength of His might'." It is only as we recognize we cannot live the Christian life in our own strength and that we begin to see that God lives in us and pours His strength through us. It was Hudson Taylor who explained that to be strong in the Lord was a matter of "exchanging our weakness for His strength."

This exchange of the strength of the Lord has nothing to do with the length of our experience. Spiritual maturity is much more than the measure of years since conversion. Paul prayed for God's strength and power for the Ephesian believers;

"The eyes of your understanding being enlightened; that ye may know what is the hope of his calling, and what the riches of the glory of his inheritance in the saints, And what is the exceeding greatness of his power to us-ward who believe, according to the working of his mighty power, Which he wrought in Christ, when he raised him from the dead, and set him at his own right hand in the heavenly places, Far above all principality, and power, and might, and dominion, and every name that is named, not only in this world, but also in that which is to come" (Ephesians 1:18-20).

The strength we receive is the resurrection power of the Lord Jesus by which He overcame principalities and powers. It is the power that defeated Satan and death when Jesus died on the cross.

Paul further reminded the believers that the same resurrection power of God is at work in us. Christian, this mighty power of God is both available and adequate for every believer in Jesus Christ. It was because of this power and strength Paul was able to say, "I can do all things through Christ which strengtheneth me" (Philippians 4:13).

Believers can know the power of the precious blood of the Lamb. "The accuser of our brethren is cast down, which accused them before our God day and night. And they overcame him by the blood of the Lamb, and by the word of their testimony; and they loved not their lives unto the death" (Revelation 12:10,11).

Believers should know the power of the Word of God. "For the word of God is quick, and powerful, and sharper than any two edged sword, piercing even to the dividing asunder of soul and spirit, and of the joints and marrow, and is a discerner of the thoughts and intents of the heart" (Hebrews 4:12).

Believers can prove the power of prayer. "Now unto him that is able to do exceeding abundantly above all that we ask or think, according to the power that worketh in us" (Ephesians 3:20).

Believers can know the power of the Holy Spirit. "But ye shall receive power, after that the Holy Ghost is come upon you: and ye shall be witnesses unto me both in Jerusalem, and in all Judaea, and in Samaria, and unto the uttermost part of the earth" (Acts 1:8, See also 2 Timothy 1:7).

The Christian soldier must stand in Christ against Satan. Paul used the word against six times in the sixth chapter of Ephesians. He had a vivid conception of the powerful forces that are arrayed against the Church of Jesus Christ. The word Paul used for "withstand" is sometimes translated "resist." That is what Peter told believers to do, "Be sober, be vigilant; because your adversary the devil, as a roaring lion, walketh about, seeking whom he may devour: Whom resist stedfast in the faith" (1 Peter 5:8,9). James also wrote, "Submit yourselves therefore to God. Resist the devil, and he will flee from you" (James 4:7).

To be able to contend against Satanic forces the Christian needs to be aware of what his standing is in Christ. Our standing in Christ denotes our union with Him and His with us. According to Paul in the first two chapters of Ephesians we are sitting with Christ. In chapters four and five we are walking with Him. Now we are standing for Him (Ephesians 6:10). Success in the Christian warfare largely depends on stability in the Christian walk. Three times Paul tells the Christian to stand and withstand against the Devil (See Ephesians 6:13,14).

What does it mean to stand and withstand?

God is able to make us stand. "Who art thou that judgest another man's servant? to his own master he standeth or falleth. Yea, he shall be holden up: for God is able to make him stand" (Romans 14:4).

We are to stand in grace. "By whom also we have access by faith into this grace wherein we stand, and rejoice in hope of the glory of God" (Romans 5:2).

We are to stand fast in the faith. "Watch ye, stand fast in the faith" (1 Corinthians 16:13).

We are to stand fast in the liberty by which Christ has made us free. "Stand fast therefore in the liberty wherewith Christ hath made us free, and be not entangled again with the yoke of bondage" (Galatians 5:1).

We are to stand fast in unity. "Only let your conversation be as it becometh the gospel of Christ: that whether I come and see you, or else be absent, I may hear of your affairs, that ye stand fast in one spirit, with one mind striving together for the faith of the gospel" (Philippians 1:27).

It takes strength to be able to stand and this strength to stand against the wiles of the Devil can be found only in Jesus Christ. When I was a young boy there were some tough gangs nearby to where we lived in South Belfast. My cousin George was a leader in one of the gangs. One day I got singled out by a group of toughs who were wanting to fight. I was no match for them, but I told them who my cousin was. As soon as I mentioned his name they let me go. Likewise, we also have the Saviour who is our Elder Brother and we can mention His name in the thick of the conflict. The Devil is more powerful than we are but we have a Saviour who is all powerful and He gives us the victory.

Standing in the strength of the Lord brings stability to our lives. It was stability and maturity that Paul had in mind when he wrote to the Ephesians, "That we henceforth be no more children, tossed to and fro, and carried about with every wind of doctrine, by the sleight of men, and cunning craftiness, whereby they lie in wait to deceive" (Ephesians 4:14). Paul found great confidence in this strength, "I can do all things through Christ which strengtheneth me" (Philippians 4:13).

Christians need to be mighty in God's strength to be able to stand like Shammah, one of King David's mighty men. David remembered him, "And after him was Shammah...and the Philistines were gathered together into a troop, where was a piece of ground full of lentiles: and the people fled from the Philistines. But he stood in the midst of the ground, and defended it, and slew the Philistines: and the Lord wrought a great victory" (2 Samuel 23:11,12).

Christians need to stand up against the Philistines in our times and against false teachings. Every soldier had to stand in his place for the battle. In like manner, every Christian needs to be standing in the place where God has placed him.

Napoleon Bonaparte made a lonely surprise visit one night to the outpost sentries on one of the vital positions of his battlefield. Stealthily he moved along in the gray light of the morning. One sentry after another immediately challenged him. Finally, the crafty warrior stole up to a strategic spot. There was no sentry to challenge him. The wily Napoleon moved closer and saw a pair of boots protruding from under a sack of corn and a rifle propped beside them. He made no comment - just picked up the rifle and himself stood guard, waiting for the awakening of the snoozing soldier. Finally the corn stirred, and up jumped the guilty defender and grabbed for the gun that was gone. Can you imagine his confusion and chagrin? It must have been a bitter and shattering experience to be caught napping by Napoleon. When the Lord of glory returns, will He find us Christians sleeping at our post of duty? John the Apostle warns that we be not ashamed before Him at His coming.

The Christian soldier must suffer hardship. (2 Timothy 2:3) Paul's picture of the Christian soldier is that of a soldier at war and not of one on parade. The day of the victory parade will come when the saints go marching in, but in this present evil world the Christian should be dressed in battle fatigues, motivated, energized and ready for action. The Christian soldier should be ready for any sacrifice he might have to endure or activity he might have to avoid that he might please Him Whom he seeks to obey.

I spent two profitable years at the Worldwide Evangelization Crusade Missionary Training College in Glasgow where we were challenged by the exploits of C. T. Studd who founded the WEC. Studd was a famed English cricketer who deserted the playing field for the battlefield of world evangelization. He used to upbraid Christians about being what he called "chocolate soldiers." In his "Quaint Rhymes of a Quondam Cricketer," he has this ditty:

Get up, get up for Jesus, ye soldiers of the Cross,
A lazy Sunday morning surely means harm and loss;
The Church of God is calling; in duty be not slack;
You cannot fight the good fight while lying on your back.

The Christian soldier must be separated to his task. "No man that warreth entangleth himself with the affairs of this life; that he may please him who hath chosen him to be a soldier" (1 Timothy 2:4). Paul has in mind the picture of a military garrison where the solider is barracked. He is ready to be called away at any moment and therefore he does not get entangled in local matters.

The Christian soldier does not run with the Devil's crowd nor should he engage in the enemy's work. God's command to His people still is "Wherefore come out from among them, and be ye separate, saith the Lord, and touch not the unclean thing; and I will receive you" (2 Corinthians 6:17).

It was said of Lord Nelson, "He was a man of one arm, one eye and one aim – fight the enemy." While the Christian soldier is called to fight he is also called to focus on one aim - to please the One who has chosen him to be a soldier.

3. The responsibility of the Christian soldier

The Christian soldier is called to be a good soldier.   What is a good soldier?

A good soldier is one who is characterised by obedience to his commander. Our loyalty to Christ is best expressed by our obedience to Him rather than simply declared by our words.

A good soldier is one who knows his objectives. The reason why the soldier of Christ chooses to obey Christ is that he might please Him.

A good soldier is an opponent of Christ's enemies. There should be no traitors in Christ's army. While we love those who love Him we must be prepared to stand up for Jesus in the face of adversity.

The Christian soldier is called to fight a good fight. "Fight the good fight of faith, lay hold on eternal life, whereunto thou art also called, and hast professed a good profession before many witnesses" (1 Timothy 6:12). As believers we are not just to fight well but as believers we should recognise also that it is a worthwhile fight. Jesus Christ is a worthy Captain and we are on the victory side. That is what makes it a good fight.

4. The readiness of the Christian soldier

"For I am now ready to be offered, and the time of my departure is at hand. I have fought a good fight, I have finished my course, I have kept the faith" (2 Timothy 4:6,7). Readiness was a watchword of the apostle Paul. He encouraged the Christian soldier to stand in the strength of His Commander, face the enemy and stand alongside his fellow soldiers in the Lord. As we shall see in our study, it is not only important that the Christian put on the whole armour of God, but he must also stand and be ready for conflict.

Furthermore, the Christian should stand united alongside other Christians to face the common enemy. Paul addressed his words not only to God's children in Ephesus but he also impressed upon them that they were all soldiers in the same army for God.

5. The reward of the Christian soldier

When Paul wrote to Timothy he wrote as a father to his spiritual son. He addressed Timothy as a teacher would address a student and commanded him as a captain speaking to a new recruit. As a fellow Christian soldier Paul encouraged Timothy to serve in Christ's army to "please Him" (2 Timothy 2:4).

In the same letter to Timothy Paul reminded the younger man of the crown that followed the conflict for those who completed the race well and fought in the good fight. "I have fought a good fight, I have finished my course, I have kept the faith: Henceforth there is laid up for me a crown of righteousness, which the Lord, the righteous judge, shall give me at that day: and not to me only, but unto all them also that love his appearing" (2 Timothy 4:7,8) .

Crowns in the Greek world were not headpieces studded with diamonds and precious stones. They were simple wreaths made from palm or olive leaves which were woven together and placed upon the victor's head as a prize for winning a race or after the conquest of war. Paul contemplated the victor's crown to be worn on the day of victory. However, we should be aware that where there is no cross there will be no crown.

There will be the crown of rejoicing for those who reach the lost. "For what is our hope, or joy, or crown of rejoicing? Are not even ye in the presence of our Lord Jesus Christ at his coming? For ye are our glory and joy" (1 Thessalonians 2:19,20).

There will be the crown of life for those who resist temptation. "Blessed is the man that endureth temptation: for when he is tried, he shall receive the crown of life, which the Lord hath promised to them that love him" (James 1:12).

There will be the crown of glory for those responsible for the flock of God. "And when the chief Shepherd shall appear, ye shall receive a crown of glory that fadeth not away" (1 Peter 5:4).

There will be the crown of righteousness for those who rally to the fight. "Henceforth there is laid up for me a crown of righteousness, which the Lord, the righteous judge, shall give me at that day: and not to me only, but unto all them also that love his appearing" (2 Timothy 4:8).

STUDY QUESTIONS

1. On what basis should the Christian consider himself to be a soldier?

2. Where is the battle against Satan fought?

3. What is the source of the Christian's strength?

4. When do you need strength to face Satan?

5. How should soldiers of the faith treat their comrades?

4

Beware of the Lion

*For we wrestle not against flesh and blood, but against principalities,
against powers, against the rulers of the darkness of this world, against
spiritual wickedness in high places.*
(Ephesians 6:12)

Among the books that I enjoy best are those that tell of the
undercover working of the Mossad, the Israeli Secret Service. For
years I read everything I could get my hands on for I found their
undercover work fascinating and intriguing.

One of the most engaging books was Our Man in Damascus
which is the story of an Israeli spy in Syria who was eventually
caught and publicly hanged in Damascus. Although he was a Jew,
Ari Cohen was an Iraqi by birth and, among other languages, he
spoke Arabic and Spanish fluently. After a purge of Jews from Iraq
he and his family were repatriated to Israel where he was recruited
by the Mossad. At the request of the Israeli intelligence agency, Ari
went to live for a while in Argentina where he posed as an affluent
business man. In his line of business he imported large amounts of
goods from Syria and as a result was invited to visit Damascus.
Through his contacts he became very friendly with top members of

the Syrian government and was even taken on a tour of the military bases of the Golan Heights when they were still in Syrian hands. He indicated to the head of the Syrian army that he would like to donate a gift of eucalyptus trees from Argentina to be planted at army bases all over the Golan Heights providing shade for the soldiers in this region which is greatly exposed to the hot sun. The offer was welcomed as a brilliant idea and a magnanimous gesture.

Later, when Israel and Syria went to war against each other, the eucalyptus trees facilitated the Israeli fighter jets in identifying the location of all the army bases on the Golan Heights giving Israel a great advantage. Observation and deftness paid off long before the war ever started.

The Mossad demonstrated that one of the most effective arms of military strategy is that of intelligence (- the study and surveillance of the enemy's strengths and strategies). Often the quality of intelligence is decisive in the conflict and eventual conquest of the enemy. On the other hand, ignorance of the enemy can prove to be perilous and costly. It was exactly this that Paul had in mind when he wrote "We are not ignorant of his (the Devil's) devices" (2 Corinthians 2:11).

Before Paul wrote about the Christian armour in Ephesians six he disclosed some intelligence about the enemy Christians are up against. While a study of "our adversary" should dispel ignorance and make us aware of his wiles, we should also be careful to not let the enemy become of such importance that we lose sight of the Captain of our salvation, the Lord Jesus Christ. There are too many today who have been diverted from focusing on Christ because of their preoccupation with demons.

Elisha demonstrated this point when the Syrian army surrounded the city of Samaria. Elisha's servant saw a vast multitude of enemy soldiers and went to the prophet crying despairingly, "What shall we do?" Elisha prayed, "Lord, I pray thee, open his eyes, that he may see. And the Lord opened the eyes of the young man; and he saw: and, behold, the mountain was full of horses and chariots of fire round about Elisha" (2 Kings 6:17). Elisha teaches us to keep our focus on the One Who is for us rather than those who are against us.

Just as it is wrong to underestimate the enemy, it is equally wrong to overestimate our adversary. If we keep our eyes fixed on the Lord Jesus, then the Devil will be kept at bay. Satan is not afraid of the sheep, but he is no match for our great Shepherd. It is for this reason that while we make a study of our adversary the Devil, we should keep our eyes on the Saviour.

When a believer becomes a child of God he not only inherits all of God's blessings and Christ's riches, but he also falls heir to God's enemies. The second Psalm reminds us that this world's system is against God and against His Christ. For some it may sound mythical to speak of the Devil. Liberals will try to deny his existence. However, if you belong to Jesus Christ, you do not need to be convinced of the reality of the Devil. You will soon discover how real he is.

The world today treats the Devil as though he were a joke or some imaginary character. I remember hearing of two boys discussing if there was such a thing as the Devil or not. One said to the other, "I don't know if I believe there is a devil or not. Look what happened when we believed in Santa Claus."

The other boy asked. "Do you think that Dad could be the Devil too?"

The scriptures do not treat the Devil lightly or as a figment of the imagination. He is a reality and has real personality. Jesus Christ spoke of him as a real personal being. (John 8:44; 12:31; 14:30; 16:11) His personality is borne out in the many and varied names given to him in the Bible.

Name for the Devil	Reference
Abaddon, or Apollyon (Heb., lit. "destruction")	Rev. 9:11
The accuser of our brethren	Rev. 12:10
The angel of the bottomless pit	Rev. 9:11
The adversary (Gk. antidikos, lit. "opponent")	1 Pet. 5:8
Beelzebub, the ruler of the demons	Matt. 12:24
Belial	2 Cor. 6:15
The Devil (lit. "one who casts through")	John 8:44
The dragon	Rev 12:7; 20:2

Name for the Devil	Reference
The enemy	Matt. 13:39
The god of this world	2 Cor. 4:4
A liar	John 8:44
Lucifer (Heb., lit. "day star")	Is. 14:12
A murderer	John 8:44
The prince of the power of the air	Eph. 2:2
A roaring lion	1 Pet. 5:8
The ruler of the darkness	Eph. 6:12
The prince of this world	John 12:31; 14:30
Satan (Heb., lit. "adversary")	Mark 1:13
That old serpent	Rev. 20:2
The tempter	1 Thess. 3:5
The wicked one	Matt. 13:19

The danger on the spiritual battlefield is that Christians do not take the Devil seriously enough and therefore fail to put on all the armour God has supplied. Paul urges the Ephesians, "Put on the whole armour of God, that ye may be able to stand against the wiles of the devil. For we wrestle not against flesh and blood, but against principalities, against powers, against the rulers of the darkness of this world, against spiritual wickedness in high places"(Ephesians 6:11,12).

In this text we can observe a plurality about the Devil's work. It speaks of "principalities...powers...rulers of the darkness." This implies that although there is one devil, there are also many demons subject to his control and working to accomplish his aims.

1. The sphere of the Devil's domain

"We wrestle not against flesh and blood...," Paul did not speak of wrestling in the sense of the sort of play acting we know wrestling to be today. It was not even a sport or a contest at the Roman Games. In the Roman world this sort of wrestling literally meant hand-to-hand combat to the death.

The Lord Jesus Christ wrestled against Satan when he was tempted in the wilderness. Paul wrestled against Satan when he was "buffeted" by a messenger of Satan. Christians today still wrestle with Satanic powers.

Paul enlightens his readers both negatively and positively about the opposition they face. First he reminds them that their conflict was not on the human level. It was not flesh and blood. Positively he reveals the spiritual dimension of the conflict is against principalities and powers. To this Spurgeon remarked, "If we fought with men we might be less guarded; wrestling as we do with subtle and spiritual adversaries, whose weapons are as mysterious as they are deadly, it becomes us to be doubly watchful lest in some unguarded point we receive wounds which will bleed for years."

In the first century the warfare was not against Nero or the Roman soldiers. It was not a battle against social ills of Roman society such as slavery or disrespect for women. Martin Luther's famous hymn, A Mighty Fortress is Our God, states clearly how cunning is our adversary:

For still our ancient foe
Doth seek to work his woe;
His craft and power are great,
And armed with cruel hate
On earth is not his equal.

This ancient and demonic foe is invisible and intelligent, but thank God he is not invincible.

Paul lists four distinct Satanic ranks in a sort of demonic hierarchy which hold allegiance to Satan:

Against principalities. This reminds us of the Devil's domain. The word "principality" carries the sense of a captain, a prince or an author. Therefore, principalities presuppose authoritative princes who have definite areas in which they rule. The Devil is the prince of all demons (Matthew 9:34). Jesus Christ said that Beelzebub was the "prince of devils" (Matthew 12:24). Demons control specific areas of our present world. (See Romans 8:38; Ephesians 1:21; 3:10; 6:12; Colossians 1:16; 2:10,15; Titus 3:1)

In Ezekiel's prophecy we read that Satan was known as the King of Tyre. (Ezekiel 28:11-19) In Daniel's prophecy we are informed of demonic spirit princes which govern nations (Daniel 10:12-13,20 Revelation 2:13).

Against powers ("Powers" = "exousia" = "authority"). Seemingly these powers are delegated authorities and this explains why the Devil can impart demonic power to individuals to work all manner of evil and deceptive works. There are supernatural demons who attack individuals. We do not know how numerous they are, but we recognise that they exert tremendous demonic power. Always keep in mind that though the Devil is powerful, he is not all powerful. Jesus Christ declared, "All power (this is the same word "exousia" = "authority") is given unto me in heaven and in earth" (Matthew 28:18).

Against the rulers of the darkness of this world. This has reference to demonic beings who have authority to rule in the demon world. They not only rule over darkness, but they also work to perpetuate that spiritual darkness. To the Corinthians Paul wrote, "The god of this world hath blinded the minds of them which believe not, lest the light of the glorious gospel of Christ, who is the image of God, should shine unto them" (2 Corinthians 4:4). It is Satan's design to hold all men in darkness by the activities of evil spirits which influence the ages. Paul warned Timothy that in the last days there will be an increase in demon activity. The Satanic doctrine of demons will not only be taught but many will believe them. It would seem that this time is already upon us. Many false cults propagate their false doctrines, and otherwise intelligent people believe the most ridiculous things.

Against the spiritual wickedness in heavenly places. Satan is not only at work in our world, but he is also active in the heavens. These "heavenly places" where spiritual wickedness operate are described by the same word used in Ephesians 1:3 where Paul praises

God, "Blessed be the God and Father of our Lord Jesus Christ, who hath blessed us with all spiritual blessings in heavenly places in Christ."

It is interesting that Paul begins his letter with all the spiritual blessings in heavenly places and draws the same letter to a close with all the spiritual enemies in the same heavenly places. In the interim Paul underlined that God raised Jesus Christ from the dead and "set him at his own right hand in the heavenly places" (Ephesians 1:20) Likewise, the believer enjoys a position in the heavenlies: "And hath raised us up together, and made us sit together in heavenly places in Christ Jesus" (Ephesians 2:6).

These unseen heavenly places find a parallel in 2 Corinthians 12 when Paul writes of the different levels of "heavenly places" when he was caught up into "the third heaven." In Ephesians 6:12 Paul refers to these unseen wicked forces at work in high places of the spiritual world. Over recent years there has been much emphasis on sinister occult activities, immoral permissiveness and an abundance of New Age mysticism which are all inspired by these demonic forces.

When we pray we penetrate the heavenlies with our supplications. Often while we engage in prayer demonic forces will oppose us. It is for that reason that we need to know and exercise the power and authority of the mighty name of the Lord Jesus Christ and the power of His precious blood. "And they overcame him by the blood of the Lamb, and by the word of their testimony; and they loved not their lives unto the death" (Revelation 12:11).

2. The strength of the Devil's devices (Ephesians 6:11)

The wiles of the Devil are the methods, trickery and deception that Satan uses. In Ephesians 4:14 Paul alludes to these wiles when he writes of the "cunning craftiness" of the Devil. Wherever there is mischief in the world, you can be sure that the Devil is at work there. The only people Jesus Christ did not tolerate were the religious hypocrites of His day, and He said to them, "Ye are of your father the devil, and the lusts of your father ye will do. He was a murderer from the beginning, and abode not in the truth, because there is no truth in him. When he speaketh a lie, he speaketh of his own: for he is a liar, and the father of it" (John 8:44). Jesus Christ taught that since the Garden of Eden, Satan always works so subtly that evil may appear as good and error might be accepted as truth.

The Devil is a destroyer who continually expresses his opposition to God (Revelation 9:11).

The Devil is a deceiver who exhibits his imitation of God (Revelation 12:9).

The Devil is a murderer who exacts death and destruction against his victims (John 8:44).

The Devil is a liar who engages in accusations against God (John 8:44).

3. The strategy of the Devil's design

It is interesting to observe where the Devil is at work:

Principally Satan is opposed to Jesus Christ. Our Lord was tempted for forty days while He was fasting. During that time Satan hurled all manner of temptations at Him as an assault on the Saviour's Messianic mission.

Satan's first temptation against Christ was to gratify personal satisfaction. This was very much a physical temptation. Satan did not tempt Jesus to commit a crime. It was more a matter of taking a short cut. Bread is a necessity of life. This was a matter of obedience and priority. Secret and personal gratification for us may not be changing stones to bread but indulging in things one should not when one thinks no one is looking. The temptation to take the convenient shortcut is universal.

Satan always suggests that a legitimate craving or desire can be satisfied in an illegitimate way. This may result in the indulgence of a selfish and secular lifestyle with no sense of responsibility or accountability. In Christ, we can win over the temptation of the shortcut in sin.

Satan's second temptation against Christ was to grasp universal domination. This was very much a spiritual temptation. This was

Satan's appeal to dazzle the Saviour with an alternative way to power. This would sweep away the necessity of suffering and death and would miraculously hail Christ in the temple court as the Messiah at the beginning of His ministry. The Devil suggested that in this way the Lord Jesus might avoid the pain of rejection, betrayal and the suffering of Calvary. "Why go the way of pain when all can be achieved so readily?"

This temptation comes to the man or woman who has been offered money or perks at the expense of a few principles. It is a seductive ploy to gain without pain in the fast lane to success. In Christ, we can win over the temptation of the spectacular.

Satan's third temptation against Christ was for the glory of public adulation. This was very much a social temptation. This was the temptation to flirt with danger and presume upon God. It draws attention to one's self and makes a pantomime of the promises and power of God.

The universality of this temptation belongs to our obsession with power and popularity. We are often more interested in impressing people than in rescuing them. In Christ we can win over the temptation of power and popularity.

Temptation in the life of our Lord reminds us that our Saviour is greater than Satan and is still able to overcome and make us to be overcomers through Him. Note what Hebrews 4:15-16 says, "For we have not an high priest which cannot be touched with the feeling of our infirmities; but was in all points tempted like as we are, yet without sin. Let us therefore come boldly unto the throne of grace, that we may obtain mercy, and find grace to help in time of need."

The temptations of our Lord also teach us that temptation in and of itself is not sin. Billy Sunday said, "Temptation is the Devil whistling in the keyhole. Sin occurs when you open the door." The best answer to temptation is to ask Jesus Christ to answer at the door when Satan comes knocking. Christ and Satan have faced each other before, and the Lord Jesus won the battle. We not only have the victory, but as Christians we have the Victor within us.

Universally Satan is against the Christless. In Ephesians 2:1-3 Paul indicates that the god of this world dominates those who are lost. They are dead in their sins. He brings darkness upon them (2 Corinthians 4:4-6). He deceives them (Revelation 12:9) and destroys them (John 10:10).

Collectively Satan is against the Church. Do not think that the Devil stands outside the church. He is very much at work on the inside. He still seeks to divide the church (1 Corinthians 1:10). He seeks to divert the church from its first love and mission (1 Corinthians 14:1-12). Satan will also seek to deaden the church (Revelation 3:1). Very soon he will try to run the church.

In 2 Corinthians 11:15 Paul warned the Corinthians to not be shocked when Satan is in the pulpit. "Therefore it is no great thing if his ministers also be transformed as the ministers of righteousness; whose end shall be according to their works." He further makes clear that the activity of the Devil against the church is extensive:
Satan is behind false brethren in the church. (2 Corinthians 11:26)
Satan promotes false apostles in the church. "For such are false apostles, deceitful workers, transforming themselves into the apostles of Christ" (2 Corinthians 11:13)
Satan teaches the doctrines of demons. (1 Timothy 4:1)
Satan beguiled believers to lie against the Holy Ghost. (Acts 5)
Satan was present when Job worshipped before God. (Job 1)

Individually Satan is against the Christian. "Be sober, be vigilant; because your adversary the devil, as a roaring lion, walketh about, seeking whom he may devour" (1 Peter 5:8). Our adversary is after every believer. When Pilgrim was on his way to the Celestial City he had to pass through an avenue of roaring lions. They were threatening and intimidating; however, he found that all the lions were chained and therefore limited in what they could do and how far they could go. They could roar but not touch him.

When Daniel knelt to pray, confess his sin and humble himself before God, it seemed that no answer returned from heaven. He had waited for three weeks for an answer from God and then he indicated what happened, "And, behold, an hand touched me, which set me upon my knees and upon the palms of my hands. And he said unto me, 'O Daniel, a man greatly beloved, understand the words that I speak unto thee, and stand upright: for unto thee am I now sent.' And when he had spoken this word unto me, I stood trembling. Then said he unto me, 'Fear not, Daniel: for from the first day that thou didst set thine heart to understand, and to chasten thyself before thy God, thy words were heard, and I am come for thy words. But the prince of the kingdom of Persia withstood me one and twenty days: but, lo, Michael, one of the chief princes, came to help me; and I remained there with the kings of Persia'" (Daniel 10:10-13). Demonic princes tried to frustrate the answer from heaven.

The Devil opposes us when we try to pray; the Devil opposes us when we do pray, and the Devil opposes us when our prayers are answered. He is our perpetual adversary.

4. The season of the Devil's deception

He knows that his time is short. God wants his children to be equipped for the warfare so that they "may be able to withstand in the evil day." That day of evil will soon come to an end. Paul already urges the Ephesians to "redeem the time because the days are evil" (Ephesians 5:16). It was disclosed to John on the Island of Patmos, "Therefore rejoice, ye heavens, and ye that dwell in them. Woe to the inhabiters of the earth and of the sea! for the devil is come down unto you, having great wrath, because he knoweth that he hath but a short time" (Revelation 12:12; See also 20:1-8). Satan is a defeated adversary who is making a last ditch effort to oppose all that belongs to God. Like a cornered animal he is fighting fiercely.

5. The secret of the Devil's defeat

With such a fierce opponent is it any wonder Paul tells us to "Stand..., stand and withstand..." while we are complete in the armour which God supplies? Some people stand on their head when Satan comes, but God has commanded us to stand on our feet. When we stand in Christ and are clothed with Christ Himself, we can resist the Devil, and our enemy will flee from us.

Although Paul repeats the word "against" six times in relation to Satan's opposition to us, he also uses the word, "able" three times (6:11, 13, 16) in which he emphasizes the great potential to overcome the evil one. God will bruise Satan under our feet and give us the victory when we stand entrenched in His strength and clothed in His armour.

The Lord Jesus gave a telling insight into how our victory is secured by Him. Jesus said, "When a strong man armed keepeth his palace, his goods are in peace: But when a stronger than he shall come upon him, and overcome him, he taketh from him all his armour wherein he trusted, and divideth his spoils" (Luke 11: 21,22). Satan is a strong man, but Jesus Christ is stronger than the Devil and has plundered hell's stronghold and stripped Satan of all his armour.

While it is true that we are surrounded by millions of demonic beings we should also be aware that God's angels do their work. The Reverend John G. Paton, a missionary in the New Hebrides Islands, told of the protective care of angels. Hostile natives surrounded his mission headquarters one night, intent on burning out the Patons and killing them. John Paton and his wife prayed for God's protection all during that terror-filled night. When daylight came they were amazed to see their attackers had unaccountably left.

A year later, the chief of the tribe was converted to Christ, and Paton, remembering what had happened, asked the chief what had kept him and his men from burning down the house and killing them.

The chief replied in surprise, "Who were all those men you had there with you?"

"There were no men there; just my wife and I," Paton answered.

The chief argued that they had seen many men standing guard and hundreds of big men in shining garments with drawn swords in their hands. They seemed to circle the mission station, so the natives were afraid to attack. Only then did Paton realize that God had sent His angels to protect them.

STUDY QUESTIONS

1. Briefly outline the various spheres of demonic forces.

2. What are Satan's goals?

3. What tactics does Satan employ to accomplish his goals?

4. In spite of a supernatural adversary, how can the Christian be confident of victory?

5. How can we prepare to stand against Satan?

5

Tighten Your Belt

Stand therefore, having your loins girt about with truth.
(Ephesians 6:14)

I am sure we feel at times that it would be a great thing if the Devil were to leave Christians alone after their conversion. The scriptures declare after all, that the Devil has already lost his grip on believers, for they have been delivered "out of the kingdom of darkness into the kingdom of God's dear Son." Nevertheless, the arch-enemy of souls refuses to leave Christians alone. As we observed in the last chapter "the devil, as a roaring lion, walketh about, seeking whom he may devour" (1 Peter 5:8). He is our adversary.

Paul's instructions to the Ephesians gives an insight of what our attitude to the Devil should be:

We are to be strong in the Lord.   God's power is adequate for us
(6:10).

We are to put on the whole   God's provision is available to
armour of God.   us (6: 11).

We are to stand against the Devil in God's strength.	Our posture is dependence on Christ (6:13,14).
We are to withstand in the "evil day."	Our perseverance is in Christ (6:13,14).
We are to quench all the fiery darts of the "evil one."	Our protection is by Christ (6:16).

There is an interesting parallel between the proper attitude of the Christian confronting his adversary in the spiritual realm and that of Joshua entering into the Promised Land. As the Christian is commanded "to stand" so Joshua was told to claim the land by standing on it. "Every place that the sole of your feet shall tread upon, that have I given you…" It was for this reason God commanded Joshua three times to "be strong and of good courage" (Joshua 1:6-9). Joshua passed Jehovah's command to the people (Joshua 1:18).

When Joshua's army entered Caanan they were not to conquer the land but to claim it. God had already given the land to Israel. After the initial claiming of the Promised Land there arose a generation that did not remember the Lord (Judges 2:10). They didn't stand against the enemy but rather bowed down to the enemy's idols (Judges 2:12). Because of this Israel was not able to stand any longer against their enemies (Judges 2:13,14.). Joshua was only able to stand against the enemy at Jericho after he learned to bow before the Lord Jehovah (Joshua 5:10-15).

To enable us to stand it is essential that we take unto us the whole armour of God. Paul advocates this should be a deliberate exercise for the Christian. It is important to observe that God has provided the whole Christian armour for the whole Church and for all time.

"Stand therefore having your loins girt about with truth." The first thing Paul instructs the Christian to do is to belt up with the girdle of truth.

1. The priority of the soldier's girdle

It is very difficult to single out any one piece of armour as having priority over another. The Christian is instructed to take the "whole armour of God;" therefore, we conclude that one piece in isolation from the rest is inadequate. Each part of armour is designed for a particular purpose and all pieces are essential for spiritual warfare. The Roman soldier's girdle was a very necessary part of a Roman soldier's armour. It should not be thought of as a mere belt. It was more like a leather apron and it was absolutely vital because every other part of the soldier's body armour depended on the girdle for security and usefulness.

Paul's observation of his prison guards in Rome let him see that the Roman soldier put his armour on and then over the top of the armour he buckled this apron. This belt held all the armour together and in place. On this belt the soldier also hung his sword and possibly a dagger, his chief implements of war.

Roman soldiers also wore a toga, a tunic or robe which was made from a large square piece of material with openings for the head and arms. The robe hung low and loose over the body. The toga could hinder soldiers going into battle as it would flap in the breeze. A loose garment would impede the soldier's mobility and fighting capacity and could possibly even trip him up. To avoid this happening the soldier took the four corners of his tunic and pulled them up through the apron-like girdle. This gave the warrior the flexibility that he needed to fight effectively. Loose fitting and unsecured armour was a handicap and could render the soldier unprepared for battle. The secure belt in place enhanced the readiness of the Roman soldier.

As Christians it is easy to become entangled with neglect and loose living. In 2 Timothy 2:4, Paul said that a good soldier should not be entangled with the affairs of this life. Just as the Roman fighter girded up his loins, so the Christian must tighten up his discipline and devotion with God's truth, or he will be ineffective in the spiritual fight.

In Luke 12:35, the Lord Jesus spoke of making sure our loins are girded. "Girding your loins" was a figure of speech which had the idea of gathering up the loose ends of the robe, tucking it into the belt and being ready to move forward. Girded loins were a symbol of readiness or preparedness for the soldier to move into battle.

After the sacrifice of the Pascal Lamb the Children of Israel were told to eat the Passover with their "loins girded and shoes on their feet and a staff in their hand" (Exodus 12:11). While they feasted on the Lamb they had to be ready for the exodus out of Egypt. Readiness is a keyword for the Christian. We also must be ready for our great exodus at death or our departure at the rapture of the saints when Jesus Christ comes for His own.

Paul spoke of being ready for death or departure. "For I am now ready to be offered, and the time of my departure is at hand" (2 Timothy 4:6).

He also spoke of being ready to suffer for the Saviour. "For I am ready not to be bound only, but also to die at Jerusalem for the name of the Lord Jesus" (Acts 21:13).

Peter exhorted all Christians to be ready to speak for the Saviour. "But sanctify the Lord God in your hearts: and be ready always to give an answer to every man that asketh you a reason of the hope that is in you with meekness and fear" (1 Peter 3:15).

Again Paul indicated his readiness to serve the Saviour. "So, as much as in me is, I am ready to preach the gospel to you that are at Rome also" We must be ready for sacrifice or service (Romans 1:15). Readiness for the Christian soldier is important.

The belt not only secured the whole of the soldier's armour, it was also used to support the soldier's weapons. He attached his sword to the belt. Significantly the last piece of armour to which Paul alluded was the sword of the Spirit, which is the Word of God. It is obvious that the sword of the Spirit is associated with the belt of truth.

2. The purity of the soldier's girdle

We might ask the question "Why did Paul say to gird up the loins? Why the loins?" The soldier's loins involved the vulnerable but vital area of his abdomen. We should bear in mind that in the Greek parlance of New Testament times the bowels were considered to be the seat of all emotions and intelligence. Peter writes, "Wherefore gird up the loins of your mind, be sober, and hope to the end for the grace that is to be brought unto you at the revelation of Jesus Christ" (1Peter 1:13).

The adversary's attack against us is often aimed at our minds which are both vital and vulnerable to the Christian life. Peter followed on from his admonition about the loins of the mind by saying, "Forasmuch then as Christ hath suffered for us in the flesh, arm yourselves likewise with the same mind: for he that hath suffered in the flesh hath ceased from sin" (1 Peter 4:1).

"Having your loins girt with truth" should speak to us of our decisive confidence in the truth, our deliberate commitment to the truth and our dedicated character which should be based on truth. What the man of God does is not nearly so important as what the man of God is. Character is shaped by the Christian's mind and it is God's truth that will ensure that we enjoy transformed minds (Romans 12:2).

Jesus Christ and Satan are antonyms. The Devil is the enemy of the truth. He is a liar; he cannot stand the truth; he cannot face the truth, and if we would overcome him, we must be committed to the truth. It is vital that the Christian soldier knows the truth, believes the truth, lives the truth and tells the truth.

The first item of the Christian's equipment mentioned by Paul was the girdle of truth, and the last piece listed is the sword of the Spirit. Both the girdle and the sword have to do with the Word of God. The order in which they are given reminds us that it is important that we wear the belt of truth before we are able to wield the weapon of truth. It is not enough to carry the sword in our hands. We must let the truth gird our hearts and minds.

Pilate asked the question "What is truth?" (John 18:38). The scriptures give a clear answer:

Jesus Christ is the Truth. "Jesus saith unto him, I am the way, the truth, and the life: no man cometh unto the Father, but by me" (John 14:6) .

God's Word is Truth. "Sanctify them through thy truth: thy word is truth" (John 17:17).

The Holy Spirit is Truth. "Howbeit when he, the Spirit of truth, is come, he will guide you into all truth" (John 16:13).

The Church is the pillar and ground of Truth. "...That thou mayest know how thou oughtest to behave thyself in the house of God, which is the church of the living God, the pillar and ground of the truth" (1Timothy 3:15).

In Paul's letter to the Ephesians he majored much on "the truth."

Christian believers are those who have trusted the truth. "In whom ye also trusted, after that ye heard the word of truth, the gospel of your salvation: in whom also after that ye believed, ye were sealed with that Holy Spirit of promise" (Ephesians1:13).

As believers we should test all doctrine by the truth. "That we henceforth be no more children, tossed to and fro, and carried about with every wind of doctrine, by the sleight of men, and cunning craftiness, whereby they lie in wait to deceive; But speaking the truth in love, may grow up into him in all things, which is the head, even Christ...If so be that ye have heard him, and have been taught by him, as the truth is in Jesus" (Ephesians 4:14,15, 21).

The Christian's testimony of a changed life is characterised by truth. "For ye were sometimes darkness, but now are ye light in the Lord: walk as children of light: For the fruit of the Spirit is in all goodness and righteousness and truth" (Ephesians 5:8,9). Great knowledge of the doctrines of the Bible is of little use unless they are framed and demonstrated in our daily experience of life.

The believer's speech is to be the truth. "Wherefore putting away lying, speak every man truth with his neighbour: for we are members one of another" (Ephesians 4:25).

Believers are those who triumph by the truth. "Stand therefore, having your loins girt about with truth ... the Sword of the Spirit, which is the Word of God" (Ephesians 6:14,17).

There is another sense in which truth refers not only to the scriptures and the Saviour, but also to the sincerity of our worship and the integrity of our walk with the Lord. The Lord Jesus taught, "God is a Spirit: and they that worship him must worship him in spirit and in truth."

At the command of God the prophet Jeremiah used a girdle that was marred and useless because it was soiled, (Jeremiah 13:1-6). God was demonstrating that He demanded truth and purity in Israel. As Christians we need to be committed to integrity. For the

Christian, integrity means you are morally pure. For the believer, integrity means you are financially dependable. Truth means you are verbally honest. Integrity means you are spiritually real. Being true means there is no fabrication and no hypocrisy in our lives. I like the contrast Dr. Weirsbie makes in highlighting the integrity of Abraham against the duplicity of Lot. The dedication of Joshua was contrary to the deceit of Achan. The spirituality of David contrasted against the carnality of Saul. The Christian is born again to be different. He should walk in the truth and rejoice in the truth (3 John 4).

3. The stability of the soldier's girdle

Although the girdle is mentioned first, it is the last piece of armour to be put on. It not only gave strength to the body it also gave support to the armour. When the girdle was put in place the soldier was ready to engage the enemy. It indicated his final commitment to the battle. Spurgeon offered this comment on this girdle of truth, "A girdle of sincerity keeps the whole man in marching order, and braces him up to meet the father of lies. An insincere man is a loose man, and a loose man is a lost man."

There are various ways to gird up our minds with the truth.

We should read God's Word. Spiritual maturity and stability cannot be known outside the reading of God's Word.

We need to hear God's Word. We can listen to the Lord's Word at church or when we share the Word together in study. "Faith cometh by hearing and hearing by the Word of God."

We need to study God's Word. Bible study is what separates those who are serious about the knowledge of God's Word from those who live on the periphery of Christian experience. God's Word is both simple and deep. Great gems are rarely found on the surface. We need to dig deep to find the most precious gems of the Word.

We ought to meditate on God's Word. As we read and study the Word of God our minds become as libraries with whole volumes of truth stacked on their shelves. By meditation we ponder the Word, personalize the Word and apply it to our lives for all situations (Psalm 1:2).

We ought to memorize God's Word. This is an investment. Jesus Christ read, heard, studied, meditated upon and memorized God's Word. Memorization will help cultivate a biblical mind. We will never regret the time we spend on memorizing God's Word.

4. The utility of the girdle.

We have already mentioned the usefulness of the girdle. However, we should also recognise that without the belt the soldier could not carry the sword. Many there are who want to wield the sword before they wear the belt. We cannot have one without the other.

STUDY QUESTIONS

1. What are the main features of the girdle of truth?

2. How should truth affect our lives each day?

3. What problems are created by failing to be truthful?

4. What attitude should we adopt to the scriptures?

5. How does Satan try to destroy the truth?

6

This Vest is Vital

And having on the breastplate of righteousness.
(Ephesians 6:14)

After Evangelist Harold Peasley and I had a meal in a West Belfast Police station we were invited to travel in a bullet-proof police car to view some of the interface areas of the troubled city. This trip took place only a few weeks after the horrendous Shankill bombing which killed nine people. As a precaution we were issued bullet proof vests to wear during the hazardous drive. After thirty years of terrorist violence in Northern Ireland we are very aware of how important and vital the bullet-proof vest is for the security forces. This protective coat has saved many lives.

On one occasion Napoleon ordered a bullet-proof coat of mail. When ready the Emperor ordered the maker to put the coat of mail on. Drawing a pistol, Napoleon fired shot after shot at the armour-clad man. Although bruised and shaken the poor bewildered man survived the severe test and was commended by the Emperor for his skill and workmanship.

No Roman legionnaire in his right mind would have ever gone into battle without his breastplate of protection. There were various types of breastplates, but the most common one was made of a molded metal plate and was tailored to suit the soldier. Roman military breastplates were also made of heavy linen covered with overlapping animal horns which were laced together. This breastplate extended from the base of the neck to the top of the thighs and covered both front and back of the soldier's torso. It was linked to and secured on the soldier by the girdle.

The soldier in battle was the target of fiery darts, and even though they were fired from a distance, they were aimed at the warrior's heart and lungs. The breastplate gave protection to all the soldier's vital organs.

At times the Roman soldier also engaged in hand-to-hand combat in which he was in peril from a swipe of a sword or the thrust of a dagger. While the soldier wore the breastplate, no sword or spear could pierce or penetrate to his chest or abdomen.

The Roman breastplate provides Paul with a parallel picture when he writes about spiritual warfare. Appropriately he calls it, "the breastplate of righteousness." This suggests to us a whole topic of truth. Just as the breastplate was vital for the soldier, so also righteousness is vital for the Christian. "Follow peace with all men, and holiness, without which no man shall see the Lord," writes the author of Hebrews (Hebrews 12:14). The girdle of truth depicts the embodiment of truth but the breastplate of righteousness is that same truth in action.

The Greek word translated "righteousness" in Ephesians 6:14 is repeated ninety-two times in the New Testament and thirty times in Paul's letter to the Romans. As Dr. John Phillips points out, "Righteousness is the theme of Romans. God's righteousness is revealed in the gospel (Romans 1:17). That same righteousness is required in man (1:18-3:23). Righteousness is received through faith in Christ (4:5) and righteousness is reproduced in the yielded life (6:12-23)."

This righteousness of which Paul speaks is the character and quality of being right and just with God. In old English the word was formerly known as "rightwiseness," the meaning of which was obvious. Righteousness is used to denote an attribute of God. "But if our unrighteousness commend the righteousness of God, what shall we say? Is God unrighteous who taketh vengeance?" (Romans 3:5). The context of this verse sets forth "the righteousness of God" as being consistent with His faithfulness and is compatible with His own nature and promises. Besides establishing the righteous character of God, Paul continues to set forth the righteousness of God in relation to the death of Jesus Christ. "Whom God hath set forth to be a propitiation through faith in his blood, to declare his righteousness for the remission of sins that are past, through the forbearance of God; To declare, I say, at this time his righteousness: that he might be just, and the justifier of him which believeth in Jesus" (Romans 3:25,26). God is not indifferent to sin, nor does He regard it lightly. On the contrary, God demonstrated His perfect holiness by satisfying all the claims of His divine justice on our sin in Jesus Christ.

The marvel of the gospel is that although God demands that we equal His righteousness, He knows we cannot. Yet, by the exercise of faith in Jesus Christ, God has provided perfect righteousness for us in Christ. Our sins were imputed to Him and His righteousness was imputed to us. "For he hath made him to be sin for us, who knew no sin; that we might be made the righteousness of God in him" (2 Corinthians 5:21).

The imputation of His righteousness to us involves the doctrine of justification and has to do with our standing before God. This was expressed in Count Zinzendorf's great hymn;

Jesus Thy blood and righteousness
My beauty are, my glorious dress!

Paul further writes, "Not by works of righteousness which we have done but according to his mercy he saved us" (Titus 3:5) This imputed righteousness of Christ to us rules out any self-righteousness. The godly prophet Isaiah bemoaned the very thought of self-righteousness; "But we are all as an unclean thing, and all our righteousnesses are as filthy rags; and we all do fade as a leaf; and our iniquities, like the wind, have taken us away" (Isaiah 64:6).

The thrust here in Ephesians 6:14 is not referring so much to imputed righteousness as it is referring to imparted righteousness. Just as imputed righteous has to do with justification and our standing before God, so imparted righteousness has to do with sanctification and our walk with God. Justification is a judicial act by which we are acquitted before God and declared to be righteous. Sanctification is the daily practical outworking of His righteousness in our lives.

The imagery of a breastplate of righteousness did not originate with the Apostle Paul. Isaiah describes the Lord, "And he saw that there was no man, and wondered that there was no intercessor: therefore his arm brought salvation unto him; and his righteousness, it sustained him. For he put on righteousness as a breastplate, and an helmet of salvation upon his head; and he put on the garments of vengeance for clothing, and was clad with zeal as a cloke" (Isaiah 59:16,17).

Paul did not limit his Christian soldier figure to his letter to the Ephesians. He also wrote to the Romans, "The night is far spent, the day is at hand: let us therefore cast off the works of darkness, and let us put on the armour of light. Let us walk honestly, as in the day; not in rioting and drunkenness, not in chambering and wantonness, not in strife and envying. But put ye on the Lord Jesus Christ, and make not provision for the flesh, to fulfil the lusts thereof" (Romans 13: 12,13). In "putting on Christ" Paul was encouraging them to display the breastplate of righteousness.

Again in 1 Thessalonians 5:8 Paul referred to the breastplate when writing about the Second Coming of the Lord Jesus Christ, "But let us, who are of the day, be sober, putting on the breastplate of faith and love; and for an helmet, the hope of salvation."

In this respect the breastplate suggests several avenues of consideration.

1. The breastplate is necessary for the perils Christians encounter

While we are in the body we are occupying Satan's territory. It is true that this is God's world, but until we arrive in heaven we will be passing through a valley of conflict. In this world Satan is forever active and aggressive towards the saints.

When Job, one of the earliest of the patriarchs, met for his devotions in the presence of God, Satan was there to accuse and slander him. Again in Zechariah 3:1 we see Satan at his usual work as an accuser of the brethren. "And he shewed me Joshua the high priest standing before the angel of the Lord, and Satan standing at his right hand to resist him."

Jesus reminded Peter, "Simon, Simon, behold, Satan hath desired to have you, that he may sift you as wheat: But I have prayed for thee, that thy faith fail not: and when thou art converted, strengthen thy brethren" (Luke 22:31).

A messenger of Satan hurled thorns at Paul; "There was given to me a thorn in the flesh, the messenger of Satan to buffet me" (2 Corinthians 12:7).

At the end of the age Satan will still be charged with being a liar and an accuser (Revelation 12:10). If Satan has been about this diabolical opposition to the saints from the earliest dawn of history and will still be engaged in the same evil work at the end of the age, then we can be sure we will not escape his assaults in our present time. "Liar" and "accuser" describe Satan perfectly. This is exactly the role Apollyon played when Bunyan's Pilgrim encountered the arch-enemy on the road to the Celestial City. Apollyon accused Pilgrim of his past sins and failures. Christian discovered he needed the breastplate of righteousness to protect him from the fiery darts of the evil one.

Satan does not fire spears and arrows at us today. He hurls demonic and deceptive teachings to lead many astray. He bombards the saints with discouragement, temptation to immoral sins and all manner of evils to make the saints fall.

There is nothing that harms the Christian more than unrighteousness. Sin in the Christian's life will destroy his peace, rob him of his joy, hinder his prayers and mar his witness for Jesus Christ. "Neither yield ye your members as instruments of unrighteousness unto sin: but yield yourselves unto God, as those that are alive from the dead, and your members as instruments of righteousness unto God" (Romans 6:13).

Is it any wonder that Paul wrote to some loose-living Corinthians, "Awake to righteousness, and sin not."

The Devil's Target. What was the Devil's target? The Christian's vital areas which are covered by the breastplate are what the Devil wants to damage.

The first target the breastplate of righteousness must cover is the believer's heart. Today we see the heart as the seat of our emotions but not so then. In the Greek culture of the first century the heart was paralleled to the mind and the will. Solomon wrote, "For as man thinketh in his heart, so is he." Again he wrote, "Keep thy heart with all diligence; for out of it are the issues of life" (Proverbs 4:23). The Lord Jesus Christ said, "For from within, out of the heart of men, proceed evil thoughts, adulteries, fornications, murders."

Charles Spurgeon added this comment about the breastplate of righteousness, "This will guard the heart. The righteousness of God, imputed and imparted, will protect the heart and blunt the edge of Satan's temptations which he aims at the soul."

It is also of the utmost importance that we guard our mind with "rightwiseness". Paul's letter to Philippians is replete with references to the Christian's mind. "With one mind striving together for the faith of the gospel" (Philippians 1:27). "Be likeminded, having the same love, being of one accord, of one mind. Let nothing be done through strife or vainglory; but in lowliness of mind let each esteem other better than themselves. Look not every man on his own things, but every man also on the things of others. Let this mind be in you, which was also in Christ Jesus" (Philippians 2: 2-5 See also 3:16,19; 4:2).

Another target for Satan's fiery darts are the bowels. The word bowels appears nine times in the New Testament and on eight of these occasions it refers to a person's feelings and emotions. Satan can play havoc with our emotions. That is why the Christian needs to walk by faith and not by feelings.

The Devil's Tactics.   What are the Devil's tactics?   Satan's primary tactics are to accuse the mind, attack the emotions and make an assault on our faith.   He will do everything to make us think, feel and believe differently from what God's Word teaches.   Our thoughts, emotions and convictions are the main factors that motivate our actions.

The Devil hurls his fiendish accusations against us.   However, sometimes he is behind accusations we bring upon ourselves or the accusations which others might make against us.   In such times we need to claim the righteousness of Jesus Christ.

2.   The breastplate provides the protection Christians enjoy

The chief value of the breastplate to the Roman soldier was to give protection.   Similarly the breastplate of righteousness is vital for the Christian soldier and it must be both sufficiently strong and strategic.   A paper bib could not take the place of this piece of armour.   The Christian needs to wear the armour of righteousness to protect the vital areas of his life.   The famous English preacher Charles Spurgeon noted, "Take notice that a breastplate is provided, but no back plate: we must never think of going back, we are bound to face the enemy, no provision is made for a retreat."

There is a well known story of a soldier who during World War II escaped certain death by the protection of a New Testament providentially placed in the breast pocket of his shirt.   He was literally saved by the copy of the Word of God.

Righteousness is everything that Satan is not.   God is characterised by righteousness, while Satan is the seat of all wickedness.   God is Light, but Satan traffics in the works of darkness.   Life issues from God, whereas Satan is the author of death.   All truth belongs to God, but Satan is the father of all lies.   Peter wrote to the first century Christians, "Dearly beloved, I beseech you as strangers and pilgrims, abstain from fleshly lusts, which war against the soul; Having your conversation honest among the Gentiles: that, whereas they speak against you as evildoers, they may by your good works,

which they shall behold, glorify God in the day of visitation"
(1 Peter 2:11,12).

We cannot escape from the holiness of God in the Bible. Among
men there is none righteous (Romans 3:10) and the very "good" that
men do is as filthy rags before God (Isaiah 64:6). However, God
demands that we be righteous (Matthew 5:20).

On the basis of our right standing before God we are exhorted to
right living. This is the work of sanctification (See Philippians 2:13
& 1 John 2:29).

3. The breastplate stimulates a vital principle in the Christian's experience

"Stand... having on the breastplate of righteousness." How can
we live without it? A Christian's life ought to be more eloquent than
his speech, and the sanctity of his soul should be much preferred to
worldly success.

We must put on the breastplate of righteousness deliberately.
You would not think of going into the day without putting on
clothing even if it were relaxed and casual dress. So must we also
deliberately put on Christ every day. Let the breastplate of practical
righteousness glint in the sunlight of your testimony every day so
that others may see your good works and glorify your Father in
Heaven. The breastplate of righteousness is simply the life of Christ
shining through your life.

We must put on the breastplate of righteousness daily. Practical
holiness should be everyday business for every Christian.
Righteousness should be reflected in the decisions we make, the
conversations in which we engage and the actions we take.

One day a young Christian came into a mission station in Korea
to visit the man who had been instrumental in his conversion to
Christ. After the customary greetings, the missionary asked the
reason for his coming. "I have been memorizing some verses in the
Bible," he said, "and I want to quote them to you." He had walked

hundreds of miles just to recite some scripture verses to his father in the faith.

The missionary listened as he recited without error the entire Sermon on the Mount. He commended the young man for his remarkable feat of memory, then cautioned that he must not only "say" the scriptures but also practise them. With glowing face, the man responded, "Oh, that is the way I learned them. I tried to memorize them but they wouldn't stick, so I hit on this plan. First, I would learn a verse. Then I would practise what the verse said on a neighbour who was not a Christian. After that I found I could remember it."

We need to learn the Word of truth and then go and translate that truth into living righteousness.

Be Thou my Vision, O Lord of my heart;
Naught be all else to me, save that Thou art-
Thou my best thought, by day or by night,
Waking or sleeping, Thy presence my light.

Be Thou my breastplate, my sword for the fight;
Be Thou my dignity, Thou my delight,
Thou my soul's shelter, and Thou my high tower;
Raise Thou me heavenward, O power of my power.

STUDY QUESTIONS

1. What are the two dimensions of righteousness for the Christian?

2. How are we protected by the righteousness of Jesus Christ?

3. How can the Christian be freed from unrighteousness? (See 1 John 1:9).

4. What might be Satan's target in your life?

5. What should the Christian do if he falls? (See Psalm 37:23,24).

7

All God's Children Need Shoes

And your feet shod with the preparation of the gospel of peace.
(Ephesians 6:15)

When my wife and I went to the Amazonian forests of Brazil in 1965 we were advised to take with us all the clothes we would need for the next four years. Among our baggage I took more shoes with me than what was necessary for that span of time, and so I brought a pair back home to wear while on furlough.

On one of the first Sundays back in Northern Ireland I preached in Londonderry and after lunch our host took us up into the mountains outside the city for an afternoon saunter. While walking up a steep incline one of my shoes fell apart. The tropics had taken its toll on the shoe and when the rubber sole parted company with the leather upper I was left flapping my foot like a lame penguin. I managed to make it back to the house, but still had to preach that night. I know the scriptures refer to the beauty of the feet of those who preach good news, but I was a preacher with one shoe on and one shoe off.

Although shoes were originally designed to protect our feet they have become a major part of our culture, mainly as a fashion item. In Roman times slaves had no shoes and wealthy people wore sandals. However, the Roman soldier needed something that was more durable and substantial than a sandal. Napoleon said, "An army marches on its belly," but we know that in reality every soldier needs good footwear. Without good footgear the soldier's actions would be severely curtailed.

So important was the soldier's footwear that Paul likens the shoes to an essential part of the soldier's equipment. A Roman soldier dared not go out into battle dressed in luxury sandals with smooth soles. In such a case he would have been slipping and sliding all over the place. The soldier needed a special shoe for fighting and a different shoe for marching, Many wars have been lost because soldiers didn't have adequate shoes.

There is a Negro spiritual which is entitled *All God's Children Need Shoes.* The Christian soldier needs to have suitable shoes if he is going to be able to stand properly. As a Christian you can have your loins girded with God's truth in your mind and the breastplate of righteousness in a godly life, but unless you can stand on your feet, you will fall. Every Christian must have a solid base.

Martin Luther stood before the adversaries of his day and declared. "Here I stand. I can do no other." His stand for the great reformation truths is not only well documented but also very much appreciated by Christians who followed Him. His "stand" for God was accompanied by some very intense times of personal conflict with Satan. Luther thought at times that the battle seemed to take on almost physical manifestations. On one occasion, in an outburst of anger at Satan, Luther picked up the inkwell and threw it at the Devil. The inkwell broke and splattered all over the wall. The stain remained for many years reminding people of how vivid was the conflict in Luther's life.

This incident reminds us again that the believer and Satan are in mortal combat. The Christian soldier should never have cold feet, but should recognise that the enemy of our souls is the same, and the weapons and armour of our warfare have not changed. We are still in combat with Satan. Inkwells are not sufficient to put this adversary to flight, but "putting on the whole armour of God that we might be able to stand against the wiles of the Devil" will.

1. The function of the Christian soldier's shoes

The Roman soldier's shoes were used for security and protection. In Roman times snares and pitfalls were laid for the unsuspecting Roman soldiers in a similar way to today's land mines. Razor sharp pointed sticks, knives and swords were concealed below the soil to injure and immobilize the unsuspecting soldier. This was a very effective strategy to impede the advance of an army, because if the soldier's feet were pierced, he would not be able to walk or run. In effect he was rendered useless and vulnerable on the battlefield. He might be a great soldier and have greater strength and skills than any other man; however, if the sole of his foot was injured, he was rendered ineffective. In order to protect their feet, Roman soldiers wore boots with heavy soles that could not be penetrated.

Likewise, it is also important that the Christian soldier has a strong soul so that he is not rendered useless.

The famous story of Achilles, the son of Peleus comes from Greek mythology. Achilles was the greatest, bravest, strongest and most handsome warrior of Agamemnon's army. One of the stories about his childhood is that Thetis, his mother, held the young Achilles by the heel and dipped him into the waters of the River Styx. Through these waters of legendary power, Achilles was thought to be invincible. He was made invincible by the waters of the river into which every part of his body had been dipped except the heel by which his mother held him. Because that heel remained in his mother's hand and had not been bathed in the river, it was still vulnerable.

It was on that very point that Achilles fell victim when an arrow sped from an adversary's bow and struck the famous warrior on his heel and killed him. To have an "Achilles' heel" indicates a weakness or a vulnerability and comes from this legend.

We all have an Achilles' heel, a place where we are vulnerable. For some it may be money. For others it may be worry, a bad

temper, selfish ambitions or a coveted position. For Samson it was
sensuality and lust. For Peter it was ambition. For Jonah it was
national pride. The Christian must be careful to protect the
Achilles' heel of his Christian life.

The soldier's shoes were used for durability and grip. Besides
having a thick sole, the underside of the soldier's shoe was studded.
Just like a football boot these metal studs gave the soldier a firm
standing and good grip on rocky terrain. A soldier in combat could
not afford to slip or fall.

Jude was confident that God was not only able to keep us from
falling but also to present us faultless before God. "Now unto him
that is able to keep you from falling, and to present you faultless
before the presence of his glory with exceeding joy" (Jude 24).
However, we must be careful not to presume that we cannot fall.
"Wherefore let him that thinketh he standeth take heed lest he fall"
(1 Corinthians 10:12). Solomon also warns "Pride goeth before destruction, and an haughty spirit before a fall" (Proverbs 16:18).

The soldier's shoes were used for mobility and speed. Roman
military footwear, although strong and durable, was a great asset to
the soldier when it came to movement. The agile soldier could not
afford to be impeded with clumsy shoes. It was important that shoes
were custom made to measure for every soldier. These shoes were
made for moving, not just for standing.

The feet that are beautiful are those that are moving to take the
good news of the Gospel to people who have never heard (Romans
10:13-15).

2.   The features of the Christian soldier's shoes

In view of the above functions of the soldier's shoes it is
important to note the principal features of the Christian who is "shod
with the preparation of the gospel of peace" (Ephesians 6:15).

This soldier's shoes indicated he was ready, prepared and equipped for war. Today the Christian must be "ready to every good work" (Titus 3:1). The preparation spoken of is not just that of the preacher's action which is expressed in Romans 10:15 "How beautiful are the feet of them that preach the gospel of peace, and bring glad tidings of good things!" Paul also addresses the attitude, awareness and alertness of the soldier servant while he is standing for God. For that reason Paul exhorts the Corinthians, "Be ye stedfast, unmoveable, always abounding in the work of the Lord" (1 Corinthians 15:58). The Christian should always be prepared for whatever might come.

The inference of the phrase, "the Gospel of peace," is that the soldier enjoys the peace of the gospel in his heart. It is difficult for the Christian soldier to engage in the work of the gospel while there is no peace in his heart. Paul tells the Colossians, "Let the peace of God rule in your hearts, to the which also ye are called in one body" (Colossians 3:15). It may sound like a contradiction of terms that a soldier at war and ready for battle must be equipped with peace, but that is exactly how it should be. The peace of the gospel should characterise the Christian's life. Peace can be enjoyed when there is full confidence in the promises of God and obedience to the will of God.

Charles Spurgeon said that we should wear the shoes of the gospel of peace, "with a happy and calm confidence, because the gospel has given us perfect peace. We shall march over the rough places of the way without becoming discontented or depressed. No pilgrim is so well booted and buskined as he who is at peace with God, his fellow-men and his own conscience."

The soldier's shoes gave stability of foot. The participle "having" which is used twice is Ephesians 6:13,14, is related to the verb "stand" which in turn gives the sense of "Stand therefore, having ... your feet shod." In Ephesians 4:14 Paul exhorts the Ephesian Christians to not be "carried about with every wind of doctrine." He prayed that they would be rooted and grounded in love (3:17). To the Colossians Paul exhorts that they be rooted and built up in Christ and stablished in the faith (Colossians 2:7).

Stability is one of the greatest needs of Christians today. Unstable Christians are not grounded in the Word of God, nor do they feed by their roots in Christ. James said that the double minded man is unstable in all his ways (James 1:8). Today we have too many Christians who do not settle in any church. Such people are blown about in all directions.

The soldier's shoes manifested his necessity for balance. "And your feet shod..." (Ephesians 6:15). Both feet are to be shod with the gospel of peace. One shoe would be no good to a soldier. With only one shoe the soldier would walk with a limp and be unsteady. He must have two matching shoes to give him balance.

We all need to be balanced in our Christian lives. It is easy to get caught up in the extremes of opposing schools of theological thought which take our focus off Christ and result in an imbalance in our Christian life.

The soldier's shoes provided mobility of step. David writes that "The steps of a good man are ordered by the Lord." The soldier who is shod with gospel shoes is in a state of readiness. He should be ready to go or ready to stay, ready to suffer and ready to serve. The prophet Isaiah speaks of feet that were active on a mission, "How beautiful upon the mountains are the feet of him that bringeth good tidings, that publisheth peace; that bringeth good tidings of good, that publisheth salvation; that saith unto Zion, Thy God reigneth" (Isaiah 52:7). Sadly there are many who are standing still in their Christian lives.

When a man asked the Duke of Wellington, "Is it worthwhile for the church to send missionaries?" the great military strategist replied, "What are your orders, sir?" We are all aware of the commands the great Captain of the Church before he returned to heaven, "Go ye into all the world, and preach the gospel to every creature" (Mark 16:15) We must be busy to fulfill that command.

The soldier's shoes suggested the nobility of the soldier's mission. God has given a banner unto those who fear Him – the banner of the gospel. There is no greater cause for which to stand, no greater Captain to follow and no greater message to deliver.

3. Fighting in the Christian soldier's shoes

Paul's instructions to the Ephesians clearly show that to fight in the Lord's battles we must stand in the shoes God has prepared for us. Paul teaches the Philippians to "stand fast in one spirit" and "stand fast in the Lord" (Philippians 1:27, 4:1). To the Romans he writes to stand fast in the grace of the gospel (Romans 5:1). To the Galatians he wrote to stand fast in the liberty of the gospel (Galatians 5:1). To the Colossians he writes to stand fast in the victory of the gospel (Colossians 4:12). To the Ephesians he writes to stand fast in the peace of the gospel and in the gospel of peace (Ephesians 6:15). When shod with the gospel of peace we are to:

(a) Seize every opportunity to serve Him.

(b) Surmount every problem that confronts us even though it be on a mountain or a desert (Deuteronomy 29:5; Romans 10:15).

(c) Stand against every foe that opposes us.

(d) Be strong for every errand on which He sends us.

The old Negro spiritual states, "When I get to heaven going to put on my shoes", but what we learn from the apostle Paul is that we need those shoes now!

STUDY QUESTIONS

1. What do the shoes of the preparation of the gospel of peace mean to you?

2. In what way do we need to be balanced in our Christian lives?

3. What contributes to spiritual stability for a Christian?

4. What do you consider to be your Achilles' heel?

5. How can the Christian enjoy peace?

8

Your Adversary the Arsonist

Above all, taking the shield of faith, wherewith ye shall be able to quench all the fiery darts of the wicked.

(Ephesians 6:16)

During the early days of terrorism in Northern Ireland the infamous "Molotov Cocktail" was a common weapon of the insurgent terrorists. It became more commonly known as "the petrol bomb." It was a terrible night in Londonderry in 1969 when the IRA rained flaming bottles down on the security forces and set buildings on fire. As the bottles filled with petrol hit the ground, the fire fiercely spread as the petrol ignited and exploded over the ground and the police. At that time the security forces were ill prepared for such attacks. However, out of that terrible experience they developed modern fire resistant protective shields which provide them with added cover against rioters and arsonists.

Satan is an arsonist. He is malicious in seeking to destroy us with his flaming attacks of temptation and oppression upon us. This is exactly what is in the mind of the apostle Paul as he continues to outline the need for the Christian to stand complete in the full armour of God.

When on duty the Roman soldier was always dressed for battle. However, he didn't employ his shield, helmet and sword until the battle actually started. As Christians we must be ready for battle at all times because our enemy is a ruthless and relentless foe. We cannot afford to overlook a single piece of armour nor to slip into complacency or neglect against this enemy.

Besides being clad with the girdle, the breastplate and suitable shoes on his feet, the Roman soldier needed to be able to cover all of this with his shield. In the hour of conflict the shield and the sword belonged together; one was used in either hand. With one hand the Roman soldier held his shield as a means of defence; with the other he held a sword as a weapon with which he attacked the enemy.

It is interesting how Paul uses the phrase, "above all." He is probably drawing attention to the shield's pre-eminent position in that it covers the breastplate and girdle. On the other hand, he might be indicating that this is the first part of the soldier's equipment to be attacked.

Paul alludes to the "shield of faith" because faith is constantly under attack. When faith diminishes, doubts increase. Furthermore, when soldiers cease to have confidence in their weapons, they discard them. Satan's primary objective in attacking our faith is to make the Christian forsake the faith. For that reason Christians need to employ the vital shield of faith.

1. **The accuracy of the Devil's weapons** - "all the fiery darts of the wicked."

Roman soldiers contended with archers in the opposing armies who used arrows with flaming rags secured to them. These rags were dipped in pitch and ignited before they were shot against the enemy. The burning pitch splattered all over the soldier's armour or where it landed, and the flame burned slowly but with great heat. Archers were fiercely accurate and could rain great havoc on advancing forces.

The shield was needed to give sufficient protection from these ferocious fiery darts. A good shield would deflect or even extinguish the arrows. Paul saw these fiery darts or flaming arrows as symbols of Satanic assaults on Christians.

Paul identifies the wickedness of our enemy. Undoubtedly Satan is "the wicked one." Paul had already identified Satan as "the devil" (6:11). The Greek word translated "the wicked" literally means "bad," "vile," or "wretched." All these names are appropriate descriptions of the great adversary of our souls. His evil design is to rob, maim and spiritually destroy us.

"The wicked" is not merely an influence or principle. Our conflict is not against a political party or some pagan philosophy. We are up against a real person and it is with him that we wrestle (1 Peter 5:8). He is unchangeably, unceasingly and militantly opposed to all that God is and all that God is doing. He bombards God's people with flaming shafts of ardent hatred and vile blasphemy against Jesus Christ and His people.

* He is opposed to the Person of God in His goodness, purity and truth.
* He is opposed to the sovereign rule of God in its extent and character.
* He is opposed to the Word of God in its authority and power.
* He is opposed to the Son of God and the programme of redemption.
* He is opposed to the people of God and God's purpose in their lives.

Paul identifies the weapons of our enemy - "the fiery darts." Besides shooting blazing arrows at the opposing army they often rained their arrows into the enemy camp to spread fire and divert soldiers from the battle front. What a picture this is of the strategy of the wicked one.

Satan has a quiver full of a wide range of malignant fiery darts which he accurately fires into our lives to arouse a flame of impure passion and lust as was seen when he tempted Eve in the Garden of

Eden (Genesis 3). He did not spare the fiery darts of fear aimed at Noah. He shot the fiery darts of greed at Lot and the flaming temptation of immorality at Joseph. His fiery arrow suggested to David that God had forsaken His people. Disappointment was aimed at Mary Magdalene; doubt was directed at Thomas; division and discord was trained on the Christians in Corinth; slander was aimed against Paul; discouragement was used against Timothy, and covetousness was pointed at Demas who loved this present world. Whatever the particular dart may be, you can be sure that by accusation and insinuation Satan will viciously aim his flaming arrows to inject his evil designs into our lives and drag us down.

Paul discloses the wiles of our enemy. Fiery darts remind us how cunning and deceptive Satan is. A dart or a javelin is something which arrives silently and suddenly and does more damage in a moment than can be repaired or healed in months. That is the reason why Paul urges his friends to "put on the whole armour of God." At times we are so busy trying to put out the fires we miss the battle.

- The flight of an arrow reminds us how suddenly Satan's attacks come at us.
- The speed of an arrow reminds us how swiftly he moves against us.
- The silence of an arrow reminds us how imperceptibly he can enter to disrupt our lives or work.
- The damage of an arrow reminds us how destructively the flame of wickedness spreads.

2. The adequacy of the shield of faith.

Christians need the protection of the shield of faith if they are to avoid injuries. The Lord promised Isaiah, "No weapon that is formed against thee shall prosper; and every tongue that shall rise against thee in judgment thou shalt condemn. This is the heritage of the servants of the Lord, and their righteousness is of me, saith the Lord" (Isaiah 54:17).

The description of the Christian's shield. The Roman soldier used two different types of shields. One was a small round shield which was strapped to the soldier's forearm. In the other hand the soldier carried his sword. This small shield was often used in hand-to-hand combat.

The other type of shield used by the Roman soldier was the "thureon" which came from the Greek word "thura," meaning "a door." This shield was a large door-like rectangular wooden board which measured four and a half feet by two and a half feet. The wooden board was covered on the outside with metal or thick leather and could withstand up to two hundred arrows in a raid.

When a barrage of flaming arrows hit the metal they were deflected, or extinguished by the specially treated leather. This shield adequately protected soldiers. The soldier could fasten this shield into the ground and hide behind it. At times soldiers joined their shields together to and form a protective barricade behind which a company of soldiers could take cover.

When we speak of the "shield of faith" we might at first think of "the faith" in the sense of the whole system of Christian doctrine. However, as well as doctrine we also need a personal and practical faith in the Word of God which enables us to overcome. "For whatsoever is born of God overcometh the world: and this is the victory that overcometh the world, even our faith. Who is he that overcometh the world, but he that believeth that Jesus is the Son of God?" (1 John 5:4,5).

The definition of the Christian's shield. The Christian's defense is the "shield of faith" and Christ is the shield that faith must apprehend and appropriate. Jesus Christ stands between Satan and us. He is our ultimate protection. We need the shield of faith every day to give us total protection. Four times in Matthew's Gospel our Lord Jesus rebuked His own for their little faith (Matthew 6:30; 8:26; 14:31; 16:8). It is interesting to study how our Saviour spoke of the degrees of faith. He spoke of faith (Matthew 9:22); no faith (Mark 4:40), little faith (Matthew 6:30), great faith (Matthew 15:28), and so great faith (Luke 7:9).

Hebrews 11 is sometimes called the "Christian's Hall of Faith." This chapter teaches us that faith allows us to believe in creation. Through faith Abel obtained redemption; by faith Noah experienced protection. Faith enabled Abraham to secure his possessions. It was faith that empowered Joseph to anticipate resurrection. By faith Moses achieved liberation of God's people from Egypt, and it was faith that brought Daniel to elevation in Babylon.

Is it any wonder Jesus Christ asked His disciples, "Where is your faith?" (Luke 8:25), and the disciples prayed, "Lord increase our faith." (Luke 17:5).

The duty of the Christian's shield. The Christian's shield will "quench all the fiery darts of the evil one." This shield covers all the other armour. To quench means to "put out" or "to extinguish." It is important to note that the shield did not just extinguish some or even most of the fiery darts; it put them all out. The shield offered total protection. We need not fall victim to the Devil's darts. Jesus overcame the fiery darts of the same evil one by His use of the Truth (Matthew 4).

The Christian's shield is faith in God. To effectively use this shield we must constantly apply to our daily lives what we believe about God, how we trust in His promises and make sure we obey to His commands. There are times when our shield of faith is the board type in which we stand together to resist and quench the fiery darts of Satan. On other occasions we handle the shield individually as we wrestle against Satan in our personal lives.

As we rest wholly in the Lord, we can know His protection. Jim Elliott was a missionary to the Auca Indians of Ecuador. One day before boarding the plane for a flight which would ultimately take him and his four colleagues to their deaths at the hands of the Auca Indians whom they sought to win for Christ, they sang, "We rest in Thee our Shield and our Defender." Regarding faith Charles Spurgeon wrote, "Faith, like a shield, covers all and is therefore important above all. Look well to your confidence in God, for if this fails, all fails."

3. The availability of the shield of faith.

Paul prefixes his instructions about the shield of faith by under-lining its priority with the words "above all." This priority does not refer to the shield alone but to the last three pieces of armour. This does not mean that the shield is the most important piece of armour. It is as if Paul is saying, "Now that you have the belt, the breastplate, and the shoes; be sure to take the shield of faith."

Although the Roman soldier had protection for every-day duty with his leather belt, breastplate and shoes, he was not ready for battle. He also needed to take up the weapons of war. Once the battle started and blazing arrows began to descend on the army, above all else he needed to take the shield, the helmet and the sword.

The verb "taking" is used in verses sixteen and seventeen: "taking the shield, - take the helmet, - and take the sword." The verb used in reference to the first three pieces of armour is "having." This related to the items that were worn at all times. However, "taking the shield of faith" spoke of immediate readiness for the hour of conflict. When the battle drew near, the soldier would take up his shield, helmet and sword. The idea here is appropriating with immediate readiness for the conflict, grasping that which is really necessary in the heat of the battle.

We have no human resources that can match the wiles and power of our adversary; however, God's mighty weapons of faith, hope, love, the Word of God, the Holy Spirit and prayer are available for us. Through God we can fight valiantly and quench every weapon formed in hell. With the weapons God has provided we can break down the strongholds of the devil. "For the weapons of our warfare are not carnal, but mighty through God to the pulling down of strong holds; Casting down imaginations, and every high thing that exalteth itself against the knowledge of God, and bringing into captivity every thought to the obedience of Christ" (2 Corinthians 10:4,5).

All the armour of God is available to us and we need to make use of it each day. No believer has an excuse for any vulnerability. It is important that as Christians we develop the ability to use the shield of faith, rightly handle the sword of the Spirit and exercise God's promises at the place of prayer. When Satan's insinuating darts of doubt, discouragement, fear and a host of other temptations come raining in on us, we must believe God and refuse to give in to the Devil.

STUDY QUESTIONS

1. What are the chief features of the shield of faith?

2. What is faith?

3. What examples did our Lord give of faith?

4. Why did Paul use the phrase, "Above all taking the shield of faith?"

5. When did you use the shield of faith? What fiery darts are hurled your way?

9

If You Want to Get Ahead, Get a Helmet

And take the helmet of salvation. (Ephesians 6:17)

We often hear it said that school teachers have a difficult profession except at Christmas and during the long summer vacation. A frustrated school teacher was exasperated at a student who appeared to be exceptionally thick. She gave vent to her feelings and roared at the timid child, "Think boy! Think! What do you think your head is for?" To this the boy shyly replied, "For putting my cap on, Miss."

Our heads are of much more use than for hanging caps and combing hair. The two most vulnerable areas for Roman legionnaires in battle were their heads and their hearts. Both had to be adequately covered and protected. A wounded soldier may be able to fight on and survive without a leg or an arm but an injury to the head or heart could be fatal. For that reason protection for both the head and heart were vital for survival.

The battle for the Christian's heart and mind is also crucial. Both are interrelated as is demonstrated in Genesis 6:5; "And God saw that the wickedness of man was great in the earth, and that every imagination of the thoughts of his heart was only evil continually."

The Bible consistently addresses both areas of the Christian's life both in the Old and New Testaments. When our Saviour quoted the ancient Jewish "Shema" in Deuteronomy 6, He said, "Thou shalt love the Lord thy God with all thy heart, and with all thy soul, and with all thy mind, and with all thy strength: this is the first commandment" (Mark 12:30). Isaiah reminded us that there is peace in the heart only when the mind is fixed on Jehovah (Isaiah 26:3). Wrong thinking leads to wrong feelings which in turn can lead to wrong actions and the wrong direction. James said it was for that reason the double-minded man is unstable in all his ways (James 1:8).

Solomon disclosed the importance of our mind and thoughts in Proverbs 23:7; "As a man thinketh in his heart, so is he." To the Ephesians Paul wrote, "Be renewed in the spirit of your mind." and to the Romans he admonished "Be ye transformed by the renewing of your mind" (Romans 12:2). To the carnal minded Corinthians Paul admonished that they bring "every thought to the obedience of Christ" (2 Corinthians 10:5).

Paul indicated that the difference between a believer and an unbeliever is that the believer has the "mind of Christ" (1 Corinthians 2:16). Having the mind of Christ is more than a theological truth. It should make a difference in what we feed into our minds. In Philippians alone Paul put so much emphasis on the thought life of the believer that he alluded to it seventeen times in four short chapters. In one verse alone he gave us seven guidelines to encourage right thinking; "Finally, brethren, whatsoever things are true, whatsoever things are honest, whatsoever things are just, whatsoever things are pure, whatsoever things are lovely, whatsoever things are of good report; if there be any virtue, and if there be any praise, think on these things" (Philippians 4:8).

The Bible's portrayal of the mind is that of a citadel, a fortress and a stronghold. "For the weapons of our warfare are not carnal, but mighty through God to the pulling down of strong holds; Casting down imaginations, and every high thing that exalteth itself against the knowledge of God, and bringing into captivity every thought to the obedience of Christ" (2 Corinthians 10:4-5).

Paul's metaphor is consistent with the constant war that is waged against the mind wherein our imagination, knowledge and thoughts are constantly under attack. We have little control over the aging process in our bodies but it is possible to renew our minds. God wants our minds to be conformed to the mind of Christ. Our love for Him should not be only with our heart and strength but also with our minds (Luke 10:27).

As we have already noted, the rebellion of Noah's day was a battle that raged in the imagination of men's thoughts which were only evil continually (Genesis 6:5). The old adage is true:

Sow a thought and reap an action.
Sow an action and reap a habit,
Sow a habit and reap a character.

It was this battle for the mind that undoubtedly was behind the Apostle Paul's exhortation to the Christian soldier - "Take the helmet of salvation."

1. The helmet God provides

The construction of the helmet. The Roman soldier considered the helmet to be one of the most important pieces of his equipment and would never go to battle without putting it on. The casing of the Roman helmet was primarily made from cast bronze which was supplemented by other metals and overlaid with pieces of leather. The helmet was designed to be comfortable and yet be a protective covering for the head and ears. It was secured on the soldier's head by a leather strap below the chin.

The protection given by the helmet. The principal function of the helmet was to protect the soldier's head and face against flying arrows from the enemy's camp or blows from the opponent's broad sword. This sword was usually wielded by an opposing soldier on horseback and was designed to strike a heavy and fatal blow to the soldier's skull.

Without the helmet the soldier would have little chance of survival or usefulness on the battle field. However, the protective covering not only provided him with a better hope of survival, it also gave the soldier the confidence he needed to engage his enemy head on.

In our time soldiers, motorcyclists, cyclists, construction workers and sportsmen all wear protective helmets because the head is still the most vulnerable part of our anatomy.

The comparison with the helmet. The Roman legionnaires were not the only ones who needed helmets; those first century Christians needed the "helmet of salvation" and we still require it today. A good helmet must be comfortable on the inside and protective and effective on the outside.

There are many facets to the Devil's attacks on our mind and we must not be ignorant of his devices. He would attack us with the broadswords of:

Doubt. According to James the doubting mind is a divided mind (James 1:6). Jesus Christ said, "Seek not ye what ye shall eat, or what ye shall drink, neither be ye of doubtful mind. For all these things do the nations of the world seek after: and your Father knoweth that ye have need of these things. But rather seek ye the kingdom of God; and all these things shall be added unto you"(Luke 12:29-31).

In prayer we are to lift up holy hands doubting nothing – not having our minds divided between doubt and faith (1 Timothy 2:8). Satan attacks us with doubts about our salvation, uncertainty about God's promises, misgivings of our Lord's mysterious providence and mistrust about His presence with us.

Someone said that a double minded man is summed up in this prayer, "Lord I crawled across the barrenness of life to You with my empty tin uncertain of asking for any small drop of refreshment. If only I had known You better I would have come running with a bucket."

Saturate your mind with the Word of God. Take the Word of God to heart and memorise it by heart.

Discouragement. At times of discouragement the author of Hebrews encouraged his readers to engage their minds and "Consider him that endured such contradiction of sinners against himself, lest ye be wearied and faint in your minds"(Hebrews 12:3). Paul was aware that the soldier can easily suffer from battle fatigue. He wrote to the Thessalonians who had faced persecutions and troubles, "Be not soon shaken in mind, or be troubled, neither by spirit, nor by word, nor by letter as from us, as that the day of Christ is at hand" (2 Thessalonians 2:2).

Elijah was shaken in his mind when he forgot how great God was and fled from the presence of Queen Jezebel. It can still happen to Christians today when we are tempted to forget God's presence with us and His assurance of victory. Paul spoke of "putting on the breastplate of faith and love; and for an helmet, the hope of salvation" (1 Thessalonians 5:8). When we are discouraged it is easy to lose sight of our blessed hope and the anticipation of our salvation.

Fanny Crosby was blind since early childhood and lived right through to ninety-five years. When she was eight she wrote a formula for her life which was titled, "Blind but Happy."

O what a happy soul am I!
Although I cannot see,
I am resolved that in this world,
Contented I will be;
How many blessings I enjoy
That other people don't!
To weep and sigh because I'm blind,
I cannot and I won't.

It took an exercise of the mind to make that decision not to be discouraged.

Deceit. Disinformation and brainwashing are favourite ploys of all military warfare and it is most certainly employed by our arch-enemy, the Devil. Paul reminded Timothy that in the last days there would be some who will teach the doctrines of devils and that even Satan himself will appear to some as an angel of light (See 2 Corinthians 11:3; 1Timothy 4:1).

Defilement. Satan wants to capture, control and corrupt the minds of Christian people. Paul wrote to Timothy and to the Corinthians to warn against the mind being corrupted by Satan (2 Corinthians 11:3; 1Timothy 6:5; 2 Timothy 2:8). Most of Satan's work in this respect is by the eye gate. We need to pray the prayer of the Psalmist, "Turn away mine eyes from beholding vanity; and quicken thou me in thy way" (Psalm 119:37).

Division. Paul pleaded with the Corinthian church to be of one mind so that they may heal the fractures and division that existed amongst them (1Corinthians 1:10-12). Much of the division among believers today renders the church ineffective in her witness because Satan has divided our minds.

2. The hope this helmet displays.

To the Ephesians Paul spoke of the helmet of salvation. To the Thessalonians he called it the helmet of the hope of salvation. Rather than finding a contradiction between the two statements Paul complemented one with the other. It is not the helmet that saves us. Without the experience of salvation we would not even be in the Lord's army.

However, this is the helmet of salvation in the sense that it is the assurance, the hope and enjoyment of this salvation in three dimensions that defends us in difficult times. A young girl travelling in a train noted that an Anglican Bishop sat across from her. Keen for the Lord and unabashed by the regalia of the clergyman the girl posed a question to the Bishop. "Are you saved?" she asked.

To this the Bishop looked up and smiled and then put a question back to the girl, "Do you mean if I have been saved in the past, or I am being saved now or that I shall be saved in the future? You see all three are true."

Salvation in the past. The believer in Jesus Christ has been saved. Salvation takes care of the past, for the believer has been saved from the penalty of his sin. Therefore there is now no condemnation for the believer in Jesus Christ (Romans 8:1). In this respect the believer was saved.

Salvation in the present. The believer in Jesus Christ is saved. God has saved the believer from the grip and power of sin. Paul reminded the Romans that they were perfectly saved now. "For sin shall not have dominion over you: for ye are not under the law, but under grace" (Romans 6:14). To the Ephesians Paul wrote "For by grace are ye saved through faith; and that not of yourselves: it is the gift of God: Not of works, lest any man should boast" (Ephesians 2:8,9). John assures us that the blood of Jesus Christ keeps on cleansing us from all sin (1 John 1:7).

Salvation in the future. The believer in Jesus Christ will be saved. One day we will experience salvation from the very presence of sin. Paul also assured the Romans, "For if, when we were enemies, we were reconciled to God by the death of his Son, much more, being reconciled, we shall be saved by his life"(Romans 5:10).

Salvation is such a complete work by justification, sanctification and glorification that we can confidently live under the helmet of the "hope of Salvation." No matter how fierce may be the battle, these truths are unshakable. It is the assurance that we are secure in Christ that conditions our mind to not give up nor give in.

This perhaps was borne out in the story of Joseph. When he was a teenager he dreamed of sheaves that bowed before his sheaf and in another dream he saw the sun, moon and eleven stars all make obeisance to him. When he shared these dreams it provoked wrath and envy in his brothers. However, when things went against Joseph he needed those dreams.

Those dreams were an antidote to doubt when his brethren turned against him, beat him and abandoned him. The dreams prevented discouragement when he was sold into Egypt. When he was tempted with defilement and lust in Potiphar's house it was undoubtedly the hope and assurance that God had a purpose for him which enabled Joseph to say no to lust. His hope stemmed from the early revelation God had given to him and these conditioned his mind for all the subsequent adversity that would befall him. Even when the full plan unfolded he confessed to his brethren, "But as for you, ye thought evil against me; but God meant it unto good, to bring to pass, as it is this day, to save much people alive" (Genesis 50:20).

3. The head this helmet protects.

Our Christian life involves our heads as much as our hearts. The first step that brought us to Christ was repentance which is primarily a change of mind. The Christian life is a process whereby the mind is renewed every day.

The scriptures urge us to strive to obtain:

A Heavenly mind.   "If ye then be risen with Christ, seek those things which are above, where Christ sitteth on the right hand of God. Set your affection on things above, not on things on the earth (Colossians 3:1,2).

A Healthy mind. "For God hath not given us the spirit of fear; but of power, and of love, and of a sound mind" (2 Timothy 1:7).

A Humble mind. "Let nothing be done through strife or vainglory; but in lowliness of mind let each esteem other better than themselves. Look not every man on his own things, but every man also on the things of others. Let this mind be in you, which was also in Christ Jesus" (Philippians 2:3-5).

A Harmonious mind. "Be of the same mind one toward another. Mind not high things, but condescend to men of low estate. Be not wise in your own conceits" (Romans 12:16).

It does not take a great mind to be a Christian but it takes all the mind that the man may have if he would be a useful Christian. A changed mind is a changed life, and a renewed mind leads to a very useful life. Spurgeon said, "He who is truly saved and knows it will wear a helm of health. The seat of thought and decision will be safe."

STUDY QUESTIONS

1. What priority should the helmet of salvation have for the Christian?

2. In what way does Satan attack the Christian's mind?

3. How are we best prepared to protect our minds?

4. What are the three dimensions of salvation?

5. What are the characteristics of the "mind of Christ?"

10

A Sword Made in Heaven

And take ... the sword of the Spirit, which is the Word of God.
(Ephesians 6:17)

The Bible is the most remarkable of all books. Here are a few amazing facts about it. The Bible was the first book ever printed. Of all books it is the most popular seller of all time and the most valuable individual book ever sold. Furthermore, the scriptures have been translated into over six hundred languages and portions of the Bible are circulated in over a thousand dialects. It rightly has been called the Book of Books.

Famous English preacher Samuel Chadwick said,

I have guided my life by the Bible for more than sixty years, and I tell you there is no book like it. It is a miracle of literature, a perennial spring of wisdom, a wonder of surprises, a revelation of mystery, an infallible guide of conduct, and an unspeakable source of comfort.

Pay no attention to people who discredit it, for they speak without knowledge. The Bible is the Word of God. Study it according to its own direction. Live by its principles. Believe its message. Follow its precepts. No man is truly uneducated who knows the Bible, and no one is wise who is ignorant of its teachings.

Another worthy said this of the scriptures,

This book contains the mind of God, the state of man, the way of salvation, the doom of sinners and the happiness of believers. Its doctrines are holy, its precepts are binding, its history is true, and its decisions are immutable.

Read it to be wise, believe it to be secure and practice it to be holy. It contains light to direct you, food to support you and comfort to cheer you. It is the traveller's map, the pilgrim's staff, the pilot's compass, the soldier's sword and the Christian's constitution. Here paradise is restored, heaven is open and the gates of hell are disclosed. Christ is its grand object, our good its design and the glory of God its end. It should fill your memory, rule your heart and guide your feet. Read it slowly, frequently and prayerfully. It is a mine of wealth, a paradise of glory and a river of pleasure. The Bible is given to us in life, it will be opened in the great Judgement and it will endure forever. It involves the highest responsibility, will reward the greatest labour and condemn all who trifle with its sacred contents.

The Bible is symbolised by many metaphors in the scriptures themselves.

- The Bible is a Light and a Lamp that shines on our way.
- The Bible is an incorruptible Seed that grows.
- The Bible is Bread that nourishes our souls.
- The Bible is a Mirror that reflects what manner of people we are.

- The Bible is a Hammer that breaks hard hearts.
- The Bible is a Fire that burns and creates heat and energy.

However, perhaps the most telling metaphor for spiritual warfare is where the bible declares itself to be "the sword of the Spirit which is the Word of God."

Spurgeon commented on this sword of the Spirit, "The Bible is a bright, keen, pointed, well-tempered weapon, for offence and defence. It cuts a way for us through all foes, slays sin, and chases away even Satan himself. 'It is written' is the terror of hell."

Most people agree that there is no other of our Lord's disciples with whom modern Christians can identify more than the Apostle Peter, the big fisherman. From his life and letters we learn many and varied lessons. One of the most important of these lessons is his experience with a sword at the Garden of Gethsemane. Malchus, one of the High Priest's guards, had come to arrest our Lord following the gesture of Judas' kiss of betrayal. As the soldiers reached for Jesus we read that, "Simon Peter having a sword drew it, and smote the high priest's servant, and cut off his right ear. The servant's name was Malchus. Then said Jesus unto Peter, Put up thy sword into the sheath: the cup which my Father hath given me, shall I not drink it?" (John 18:10,11).

Peter made the mistake of trying to fight a spiritual battle with a physical weapon. He engaged the wrong enemy, with the wrong weapon, at the wrong time and in the wrong place. This lesson was well learned, for on the day of Pentecost he stood before an agitated multitude of thousands in Jerusalem and in spite of the enemies of the Saviour, Peter wielded no other weapon apart from the sword of the Spirit. As a result thousands of men and women were pricked in their hearts.

This is a lesson for us all to learn. Paul already stated that we do not wrestle with flesh and blood. We are up against dark spiritual forces. Carnal weapons are futile in our fight against our spiritual enemy. The sword of the Spirit, which is the Word of God, is provided in the heavenly arsenal.

In history we read about the sword and the Koran in the spread of Islam after the death of Mohammed in the eighth century. Much blood was spilled as Islam was imposed on nations. The human sword cannot compare to the sword of the Spirit. God's work prospers by this tool which God made in heaven and revealed on earth.

The author of Hebrews declared, "For the Word of God is quick, and powerful, and sharper than any two-edged sword, piercing even to the dividing asunder of soul and spirit, and of the joints and marrow, and is a discerner of the thoughts and intents of the heart" (Hebrews 4:12). On the basis of this verse we are able to conclude that the physical sword is dead, but the sword of the Spirit is living; a physical sword penetrates only the body dividing flesh and bones, but the sword of the Spirit penetrates the heart dividing between soul and spirit; the carnal sword stabs living men to death but the sword of the Spirit stirs dead men to life.

The sword is the sixth piece of armour for the Christian soldier. Until now all that we have considered in Paul's description of the Christian soldier has been defensive. A sword is an assault and offensive weapon for attacking an enemy. However, for a soldier to have offensive weapons without defensive armour would leave him very vulnerable. On the other hand, armour without weapons would render the soldier useless. For that reason Paul urged that the Christian take unto himself "the whole armour of God."

1. The making of the sword of the Spirit

The model of the Roman sword. Paul not only surveyed the armour of the Roman soldier but also his arsenal. Roman legionnaries were skillful soldiers both in the use of the broad sword and the long sword. They also learned to wield a shorter and more narrow dagger-like weapon. The Greek word used here for "sword" is "machaira" The same word is also used in Matthew 26:47,51; Acts 12:2; and Hebrews 11:37 where it always refers to the common two-edged sword which was used by most soldiers. This could have been anything from the short six-inch dagger to the eighteen-inch sword. The sword was carried in sheath or a scabbard attached to the soldier's belt and hung at his side. This weapon was used specifically in hand-to-hand combat and is consistent with Paul's use of "we wrestle" which also infers close combat with the enemy.

The mystery of the divine sword. When Paul spoke of "the sword of the Spirit" there are various strands of truth implied. The phrase, "sword of the Spirit," suggests ownership, for it is the sword which belongs to the Holy Spirit. Sword of the Spirit also suggests the origin, for it not only belongs to Him but the scriptures were produced by the Holy Spirit. The same term, "sword of the Spirit," can also imply that it is the weapon which is used by the Spirit. A sword is of no use or function unless it is used, and most certainly the Holy Spirit uses this sword. It is by the Word of God and operation of the Holy Spirit that we are born again (1 Peter 1:23).

The scriptures are owned by God. "Jesus answered them, Is it not written in your law, I said, Ye are gods? If he called them gods, unto whom the word of God came, and the scripture cannot be broken" (John 10:34,35).

The scriptures originated with God. "All scripture is given by inspiration of God, and is profitable for doctrine, for reproof, for correction, for instruction in righteousness: That the man of God may be perfect, throughly furnished unto all good works" (2 Timothy 3:16,17).

The scriptures are used by God. "For the Word of God is quick, and powerful, and sharper than any two-edged sword, piercing even to the dividing asunder of soul and spirit, and of the joints and marrow, and is a discerner of the thoughts and intents of the heart" (Hebrews 4:12).

The miracle of the Spirit's sword. This Bible is a miracle book. It is Divine in its origin. It is the Word of God. In this book there are forty different writers who produced sixty-six books, written over a period of one thousand six hundred years in different countries yet there is only one Author, the Holy Spirit, and they all have one common theme which is Jesus Christ (See Luke 24:44).

The phrase, "the Word of God," is the Bible's most frequently used designation of the scriptures. In the first five books "God said…" is repeated seven hundred times. Four thousand times in the Old Testament we read, "The Word of the Lord." It all testifies that when the Bible speaks, God speaks. According to 2 Timothy 3:16 "Every Word of God is inspired and proceeds from the mouth of God…" Because it is inspired it must also be inerrant, for God cannot lie. Because it is inerrant it is infallible, for it cannot fail. Because it is infallible then it is immutable, for it cannot change. The Bible undoubtedly is the very Word of God.

Of course, some will tell us that the Bible contains the Word of God, or it becomes the Word of God as it speaks to us. We maintain that "All scripture is given by inspiration of God, and is profitable…." Continuously and consistently the Bible is the Word of God irrespective of our consent or co-operation.

2. The marks of the sword of the Spirit

The writer to the Hebrews spoke clearly of this sword of the Spirit. "For the Word of God is quick, and powerful, and sharper than any two-edged sword, piercing even to the dividing asunder of soul and spirit, and of the joints and marrow, and is a discerner of the thoughts and intents of the heart" (Hebrews 4:12).

The Word of God is living. It pulsates with life. The Lord Jesus said to His disciples, "The words that I speak unto you, they are spirit, and they are life" (John 6:63). His Word is life for He Himself is the life. The Bible is living in its words and content for it is all about the living Lord Jesus who is also called the Word of God (See Revelation 19:13).

The Word of God is also life-giving. This wonderful book has the energy to kill or to heal. It has the power to take life or to give life. James said, "Of his own will begat he us with the word of truth" (James 1:18). Peter stated that the Christian is a person who has been "Born again, not of corruptible seed, but of incorruptible, by the Word of God, which liveth and abideth for ever"(1 Peter 1:23). The Word of God is the only book that can quicken men and women and bring about a great revival.

The Word of God is lasting. The Word of God is timeless, deathless and everlasting. It will never wear out nor will it ever wear done. Skeptic, critics, cynics and clerics could never destroy it. Just like many hammers are worn out while the anvil outlasts them all, so also the Word of God will outlive all other books and writings.

A young Italian girl sat at her fruit stand intently absorbed in reading a small book. A gentleman, pausing to get some fruit, asked her what she was reading with so much interest. She replied, rather timidly, "The Word of God, Sir."

But he was one who called himself a skeptic. He said, 'Who told you the Bible was the Word of God?'

With childish simplicity she replied, "God told me Himself."

"God told you? Impossible! How did He tell you? You have never seen Him nor talked with Him. How could He tell you?" insisted the skeptic.

For a few moments the girl was confused and silent. Then looking up, she said respectfully, "Sir, who told you there is a sun in the sky up there?"

The man replied, rather contemptuously, "Who told me? Nobody; I don't need to be told. The sun tells this about itself. It warms me. I love its light."

To this the young Italian girl earnestly answered, "You have put it straight, sir, for the sun and the Bible. I read it. It warms my heart. It gives me light. I love its light and its warmth. None but God could give the light and warmth I get from this Book."

The man turned away quietly, embarrassed by her simple faith.

3. The ministry of the sword of the Spirit.

The Word of God is engaged in an active ministry. It is powerful and energetic. When God spoke in Genesis 1 the planets moved through space, the sun shone in the heavens and stars twinkled at night time. When Jesus spoke, disease fled, death retreated and storms ceased to blow. Three thousand years ago David wrote, "The law of the Lord is perfect, converting the soul: the testimony of the Lord is sure, making wise the simple. The statutes of the Lord are right, rejoicing the heart: the commandment of the Lord is pure, enlightening the eyes. The fear of the Lord is clean, enduring for ever: the judgments of the Lord are true and righteous altogether."

The scriptures have power today. According to the Psalmist the Word of God has the power to convict of sin. On the Day of Pentecost when sinners heard the Word of God they were pricked in their hearts by the sword of the Spirit and confessed their sins. This Word cuts the heart. It penetrated and cut the heart of Saul the persecutor of the church and the hearts of Roman guards in the palace of the Emperor.

The Word of God has power to convert the soul to Jesus Christ. Paul declared, "Faith cometh by hearing, and hearing by the Word of God" (Romans 10:17). It is the Word of God that produces faith.

The Bible has power to cleanse from sin. Jesus said, "Now ye are clean through the Word I have spoken unto you" (John 15:3).

The Word of God has power to comfort the sorrowing. Paul wrote to the young Christians in Thessalonica "Wherefore comfort one another with these words" (1 Thessalonians 4:18).

The Word of God has power to conquer Satan. During His earthly life our Lord Jesus repeatedly and effectively used the sword of the Spirit to conquer Satan in the Wilderness. In Revelation 19:15 we read "Out of his mouth goeth a sharp sword, that with it he should smite the nations." God has given us this mighty weapon.

4. The mastery of the sword of the Spirit.

A sword was of no use if it was not employed and engaged in battle. Writing concerning what she called, "God's perfect weapon," Corrie Ten Boom said, "As the Lord Jesus used this sword to overcome the evil one in His temptation experience, so we must learn to defend ourselves against every sort of attack."

Today swords adorn the walls of museums or are used for ceremonial occasions on parade grounds. Not so with the sword of the Spirit. It is active today and Christians need to be mastered by the sword as well as adept in using it. For that reason Paul commanded that the Christian soldiers "take the sword of the Spirit."

When Nehemiah was building the walls of Jerusalem he commanded that every man had his sword girded by his side as they builded (Nehemiah 4:17-19). His men were ready both for the building of the walls and to battle in the war. That is the pattern we need to follow today. Christians today do not need to store the sword of the Spirit in a sheath at their side. The Word of God is to be hidden in our hearts and spoken with our mouths.

We need to understand the sword of the Spirit -
Know the Book

We need to trust the sword of the Spirit -
Believe the Book

We need to be skilful with the sword of the Spirit -
Act on the Book

Our desires for God's Word can be no greater than were David's desire for the saints in his day, "Let the high praises of God be in their mouth, and a two-edged sword in their hand" (Psalm 149:6).

STUDY QUESTIONS

1. Why should Paul refer to the scriptures as the "sword of the Spirit?"

2. What characteristics give evidence that the Bible is a miracle book?

3. What practical power has the Word of God?

4. Memorize a name for Christ from each book of the Old Testament.

5. How may the Christian use the Word of God each day?

11

The Canopy of Prayer

*Praying always with all prayer and supplication in the Spirit, and
watching thereunto with all perseverance and supplication for all saints;
And for me, that utterance may be given unto me, that I may open my
mouth boldly, to make known the mystery of the gospel.*
(Ephesians 6:18,19)

Just before Britain's Princess Diana was tragically killed in Paris in
1997 she made a much publicized visit to war-ravaged Angola in
conjunction with the Red Cross campaign to abolish the use of
landmines. Always conscious of her personal beauty and public
image the princess was impressively dressed in casual clothes as
she accompanied an ordinance soldier to detonate a land mine.
Though the princess added much publicity to the worthy campaign
even she had to wear a specially designed protective apron and
helmet to shield her from any accidental injury. The transparent
apron worn on top of Diana's coordinated clothes not only protected
the pretty princess, but also allowed her beauty to shine through and
enhance her image.

The Christian needs not only to be dressed for battle, but he also
needs to be covered over with an apron of prayer. It seems that
Paul referred to this over all protection in the climax he gives to the

Christian's armour.   Paul stresses four "alls" when it comes to the matter of prayer. "Praying *always* with *all prayer* and supplication in the Spirit, and watching thereunto with *all perseverance* and supplication for *all saints*;" Paul is pointing to the central role that prayer should play in all of our lives, all of the time.

As we have studied the "Christian Soldier" we notice that Paul first instructed the believer to detect the adversary (Ephesians 6:12) and to dress for battle (6:13-17).   He crowns this by teaching us how we may destroy the wiles of the Devil by using God's weapons for the warfare (6:17,18).

The weapons for spiritual warfare are not carnal.   Carnal weapons are not suitable for spiritual conflict. For that reason Paul insisted that beyond our spiritual clothing we must be armed with "the sword of the Spirit which is the Word of God: praying always in the Holy Spirit."   Just as we cannot separate the sword from the rest of the armour so we dare not separate the Word of God from prayer.   It is by the Word of God that we are spiritually enlightened and by prayer that we are spiritually enabled.   Prayer is not a substitute for spiritual armour.   It is a support to our armour.

In Ephesians 3:14 we find prayer is an expression of worship by God's children.   Jim Elliott said, "God is still on the throne and we are still at His footstool and there is only a knee's distance between."

Prayer is the work of God's servants (Ephesians 1:16-23).

Prayer is a weapon of war for God's soldiers (Ephesians 6:18).

If the girdle, breastplate, shoes, shield and helmet are the armour the soldier wears, prayer is the vital air the Christian breathes. The use of the verb "praying" indicates to us that "standing our ground" and "taking our armour" are all done by "praying."

Put on the gospel armour,
Each piece put on with prayer;
Where duty call or danger
Be never wanting there.

Prayer is vital to our equipment.   Prayer keeps the Christian's armour bright.   Mr. Spurgeon's comment on this verse is, "This weapon of all prayer will often serve our turn when all others are out of our reach. So long as we can pray we shall not be overcome." Let us then look at the "overalls" of prayer.

1. The "all" of the frequency of prayer. – Praying always

"Always" here means "at all seasons" or "on all occasions." We are to pray when we are in the midst of a spiritual battle. Often when we are in the thick of a conflict we do not feel like praying or feel we cannot pray. At such times we should pray in spite of our feelings. Our faintest and feeble requests are presented perfectly by the Holy Spirit even when we do not know how to pray. "Likewise the Spirit also helpeth our infirmities: for we know not what we should pray for as we ought: but the Spirit itself maketh intercession for us with groanings which cannot be uttered" (Romans 8:26).

Therefore, we ought to pray when we think things are going well and continue to pray when it seems things are not going well. In other words, just as in the marriage vows, we should pray for better, pray for worse, pray for richer, pray for poorer, pray in sickness and pray in health. Pray always.

This teaches us that prayer in the Christian's life should be:

Continual prayer. Living in an attitude and atmosphere of prayer. (Matthew 18:1)

Habitual prayer. Cultivate the habit of regular prayer times.

Special prayer. Special situations require special seasons of prayer (Acts 1 & 12)

Failure to pray is not only a tragedy, it is a sin against God. With this in mind Samuel promised Israel, "Moreover as for me, God forbid that I should sin against the Lord in ceasing to pray for you" (1 Samuel 12:23).

2. The "all" of the facets of prayer - "With all prayer and supplication in the Spirit"

"Prayer" is a general term, but those who engage in it must learn there are many facets to prayer. It was in the context of spiritual warfare that Paul wrote to Timothy, "That thou by them mightest war a good warfare; holding faith, and a good conscience;...I exhort therefore, that, first of all, supplications, prayers, intercessions, and giving of thanks, be made for all men" (1Timothy 1:18,19; 2:1).

This verse suggests the following:

"I exhort..." We pray because we are commanded to pray.

"...First of all..." God puts prayer as a priority in our lives. (See Luke 18:1 Acts 12:5). Prayer should be the first thing we do and not be left as the last resort. John Bunyan, author of Pilgrim's Progress, said, "You can do more than pray after you have prayed, but you cannot do more than pray until you have prayed."

"...Supplications..." Supplication is very much the human aspect of prayer. It reflects who we are. This word suggests the petitioner is poor and needy and out of that sense of need we come to ask of God as the great Benefactor and our heavenly Father.

"...Prayers..." This is the divine aspect of prayer. It reflects Who God is and underscores our confidence in God's sufficiency and power. True prayer is based on the relationship between the needy sinner and the heavenly Father.

"...Intercessions..." When we pray for others we intercede. In the Body of Christ we are encouraged to pray for each other. This is greatly demonstrated by Paul when he wrote to the Thessalonians and assured them of his prayers for them (2 Thessalonians 1:11). Before the end of the letter he appeals to the believers to pray for him (2 Thessalonians 3:1). We also intercede when we pray for those who cannot pray for themselves. Oswald Sanders said, "It is possible to move men through God by prayer alone."

"...Giving of thanks..." Thanksgiving is the acknowledgment that God answers prayer. We should not pray without giving thanks. Spurgeon said that prayer and praise are next-of-kin to each other. (See Philippians 4:6)

Someone suggested using the word "ACTS" as an acrostic in prayer. Adoration, Confession, Thanksgiving and Supplication.

3. **The "all" of fervency in prayer** - "in the Spirit, and watching thereunto with all perseverance"

"Prayer and supplication in the Holy Spirit." It has been said that the prayer that reaches heaven is the prayer that originates in heaven. The Holy Spirit understands our weaknesses on earth so He energizes us for prayer. He also understands God's will for us so he enlightens us in prayer. "Likewise the Spirit also helpeth our infirmities: for we know not what we should pray for as we ought: but the Spirit itself maketh intercession for us with groanings which cannot be uttered" (Romans 8:26).

By prayer the Holy Spirit imparts His desires to our hearts. He opens up the avenues of our souls and controls our minds, shapes our wills according to His Word and leads us in our prayers. Prayer is a relationship by which we pray to our heavenly Father, "Speak Lord for your servant hears. Listen for your servant speaks."

"Watching" is a military term appropriate to an alert sentry on duty. The Christian should be a soldier on watch with unwearied persistence. To watch is to be alert. Always keep on praying even when it seems the answer will not come. It is said that George Muller prayed for an unconverted man in Bristol for sixty-five years and the man was converted only after Muller died. That is perseverance.

Watching also involves perception. By watching we should endeavour to see what God sees and feel what He feels. By watching we begin to see things from God's point of view.

Watching implies perseverance also. According to the parables of our Lord in Luke 11 we are to have importunity in our prayers. Importunity is perseverance and persistence at prayer, reflect a confidence in God that refuses to give up. Persistence in prayer is to ask and keep on asking of God.

The night Jesus was arrested in the Garden of Gethsemane, Peter and the other disciples fell asleep when they should have been praying. They lacked perseverance. They were not the last people to fall asleep at prayer. All of us need to make prayer a priority and always keep on praying, no matter how full our schedule may be.

4. The "all" of focus in prayer - "for all saints… and for me"

We are encouraged to pray for all saints in general. We can never attach too much importance to prayer. Even an apostle needed the prayers of the saints. Keep on praying "for all the saints." It is good to pray for our family, our friends and for our own needs. But Paul says that our list needs to be longer. We need to pray for all the saints.

Paul practised what he preached. In Ephesians 3:14-21 he prayed for the Ephesian believers in one of the most fervent, comprehensive and sublime prayers of the Bible. It is a good exercise to use the Psalms to pray personal prayers. We might also use Ephesians 3:14-21 as a guide to praying for other Christians.

Remember again that Paul was in prison as he wrote this letter. He was thinking on the needs of others even though he was suffering persecution. Paul was a selfless servant of God. It is true that as we pray for others our very prayers become a blessing to us. "And the LORD turned the captivity of Job, when he prayed for his friends: also the LORD gave Job twice as much as he had before" (Job 42:10).

We are urged to pray for some saints as individuals. "And for me." Paul moved from the appeal for general prayer to a specific prayer request that he had. He wanted the Ephesian believers to pray for him.

The specific request that Paul had in mind was that God would enable him to have boldness and clarity in telling others about Christ. He desired God's help to faithfully proclaim the great news that the Lord will grant salvation to all those who trust in Jesus Christ. It is interesting that Paul called himself "an ambassador in bonds." This alludes to the fact that as he wrote this letter, he was a prisoner in a Roman dungeon.

I am impressed that Paul did not ask the Ephesian Christians to pray for his release. He requested prayer for opportunity rather than liberty. I must confess that if I were in a Roman dungeon I also would ask people to pray for me. However, I think I would ask them to pray for something else other than an opportunity to preach. I would probably want them to make it a priority to pray that God would get me out of the prison - fast. I am sure Paul would not have objected if God had sent a couple of angels to spring him out of prison, as He had done for Peter in Acts 12, but he did not pray for that.

Paul could have listed different things for which he wanted others to pray to improve his quality of life. Yet, his priority, his most important concern, was that he would be an effective ambassador for Jesus Christ and that is what he asked his friends to pray for.

Prayer provides an opportunity for each of us to be involved in the ministry of others. When Paul was preaching in Asia and was up against great difficulties in his ministry, he assured the Corinthian Christians that they also had been helpers together with him in their prayers to God for him. (2 Corinthians 1:8-11). You can travel the world through prayer and aid God's servants in all places by your intercessions.

I must confess that I do not understand how prayer works any more than I understand how electricity works. I know that prayer changes things and people too. A church or a life without prayer is about as valuable as a light bulb without electric power.

In the late eighteenth century an American pastor was in London and visited the famous Metropolitan Tabernacle, the church which was pastored by Charles Spurgeon. The world-famous preacher offered to give his American guest a tour of the building. After a few minutes, Spurgeon said to his guest, "Now let me take you downstairs to show you our power plant."

The American pastor expected to see a coal-powered generator, but instead Spurgeon took him to a room where two hundred people were meeting on Friday evening, praying for the Sunday worship services.

Evangelist James Stewart wrote of Spurgeon, "So greatly did this brilliant man depend on God that he made prayer meetings the order of the day. His whole church work was honeycombed with prayer. It is said that five to six hundred people were on their knees in another room every time he preached. On Monday nights, some three thousand souls gathered to pray God's richest blessing on the Word preached to the vast audiences on the Sunday."

That was the secret of real power in Spurgeon's ministry and remains the secret of blessing in the lives of all those who engage in service for Jesus Christ.

Until our Saviour comes again all Christians are called to spiritual conflict. As well as standing in the strength of the Lord and putting on all the spiritual armour prepared for us, we must combat the enemy of our souls by the means of grace provided for us the sword of the Spirit and the "overalls" of prayer.

When I was a student at the WEC Missionary Training College in Glasgow we were greatly challenged by missionaries returning from distant lands where they had engaged on difficult and sometimes dangerous missions of sacrificial service for the Lord Jesus Christ. As we faced the challenge to follow their example we learned to prayerfully sing Amy Carmichael's prayer:

> *From prayer that asks that I may be*
> *Sheltered from winds that beat on Thee,*
> *From fearing when I should aspire,*
> *From faltering when I should climb higher,*
> *From silken self, O Captain, free*
> *Thy soldier who would follow Thee.*
>
> *From subtle love of softening things,*
> *From easy choices, weakenings,*
> *Not thus are spirits fortified,*
> *Not this way went the Crucified.*
> *From all that dims Thy Calvary,*
> *O Lamb of God, deliver me.*
>
> *Give me the love that leads the way,*
> *The faith that nothing can dismay,*
> *The hope no disappointments tire,*
> *The passion that will burn like fire,*
> *Let me not sink to be a clod;*
> *Make me Thy fuel, Flame of God*

STUDY QUESTIONS

1. Why should prayer be a priority?

2. What are the various facets of prayer?

3. Why should we persevere in prayer?

4. Draw up a daily prayer plan that will enable you to travel the world in prayer.

5. Set prayer targets. List ten neighbours or friends for whom you will pray.

12

Energized and Equipped

Be not drunk with wine, wherein is excess; but be filled with the Spirit.
(Ephesians 5:18)

Throughout this study we have been considering the heavenly armour God has provided for the Christian soldier as the equipment Christians must use. We conclude this study focusing on the ability and energy of the Christian soldier to effectively and successfully wage warfare. Paul stressed not only our engagement in the war but also our victory in the conflict when he exhorted "Be strong in the Lord and in the power of His might."

We do well to ask "How can we be strong or strengthened for the battle against temptation, doubt and fear which we meet every day?" The letter which Paul wrote from a Roman prison to the Ephesians provides us with the answer to that question, "Be not drunk with wine, wherein is excess; but be filled with the Spirit" (Ephesians 5:18).

Years ago I learned that one of the most profitable methods of Bible study is to approach a verse or a portion of Scripture as though you were entering a house. The first thing to look for is the key word to open the door that will unlock the principal truth of the portion. Having found that key word employ the help of a good concordance or a computer Bible programme to trace the thread of truth through the whole Bible. You will discover that the Bible is the best commentary on the Bible.

Employing this method in Ephesians reveals the presence and pre-eminence of the Holy Spirit throughout Paul's letter and is an essential factor in equipping the Christian soldier in complete armour to be ready for spiritual conflict.

Observe Paul's reference to the Holy Spirit in every chapter of Ephesians:

1:13   "Sealed with that Holy Spirit of promise."

1:17   "The Spirit of wisdom and revelation..."

2:18   "...access by one Spirit unto the Father."

2:22   "Builded together for an habitation of God through the Spirit."

3:5   "Revealed unto....apostles and prophets by the Spirit."

3:16   "Be strengthened with might by His Spirit."

4:3   "Endeavouring to keep the unity of the Spirit."

4:4   "There is one Body and One Spirit."

4:30   "Grieve not the Holy Spirit of God, whereby ye are sealed unto the day of redemption."

5:9   "For the fruit of the Spirit is in all goodness and righteousness and truth."

5:18   "Be filled with the Spirit."

6:17   "And the sword of the Spirit, which is the Word of God."

6:18   "All prayer and supplication in the Spirit."

These references teach us that the life, unity, wisdom, strength and energy of the church and the individual Christian wholly depend on the personality, presence, power and work of the Holy Spirit. He is the Divine Comforter who has come in the place of Christ, revealing Christ to us and making us to be Christlike.

Out of these many references I suggest that we pick up two strands of truth that are paramount in Ephesians.

* The Holy Spirit's residence in us. "Ye also are builded together for an habitation of God through the Spirit" (2:22).

* The Holy Spirit's fullness in us. "Be filled with the Spirit" (5:18).

When we speak of the residence of Spirit we are reminded that we are but "temples" in which God dwells. When we think of the fullness (being filled) of the Spirit we are reminded that God dwelt not only in the temple at Jerusalem but when Solomon fully dedicated that Temple to the Lord He filled the Temple with His glory (See 1 Kings 8:10,11).

Sadly, although all Christians are indwelt by the Holy Spirit not all Christians are filled with the Holy Spirit. Many fail to enjoy and experience this fullness either because of ignorance, disobedience or fear. The Spirit-filled Christian is a supernatural living person and not "a super limited edition" of a removed saint. It can be and should be the normal Christian life.

Many of the commands Paul gave to the Ephesians were general commands to all the Christians in that church. However, when he addressed the matter of being filled with the Holy Spirit he spoke individually to every Christian in the church.

Why should I be filled with the Holy Spirit? Let me suggest four good reasons why the Christian needs to be filled with the Holy Spirit.

1. Because of obedience to God's Word.

This fullness of the Holy Spirit is not an option or a suggestion. It is a command we must obey. Paul's command was imperative, "Be filled with the Spirit." The command is not to be baptized with the Spirit or by the Spirit. When Jesus Christ spoke of baptism by the Spirit he never spoke of it as a command but as a promise to be fulfilled, "Ye shall be baptized with the Holy Ghost not many days hence" (Acts 1:5). This promise was realized for the apostles at Pentecost and for every Christian when they are baptized into the body of Jesus Christ. "For by one Spirit are we all baptized into one body, whether we be Jews or Gentiles, whether we be bond or free; and have been all made to drink into one Spirit" (1 Corinthians 12:13).

There are many who disagree with this interpretation of the fullness of the Holy Spirit, but, I would much prefer that people differ about the terminology of the Spirit's fullness than to claim to have the right terms and live in dead orthodoxy without that fullness.

"And be not drunk with wine, wherein is excess; but be filled with the Spirit." Paul's imperative does not refer to the filling of the Holy Spirit alone. The negative of his command forbids alcoholism while the positive relates God's provision for supernatural living. To obey one part of Paul's injunction and neglect the other results in failure to obey God. Disobedience to the command of the Spirit's fullness is a sin just as much as being drunk is a sin.

The church where I pastor would be scandalized if I were to arrive drunk in the pulpit or if the office bearers were to be found drunk during the week, and rightly so. However the verse that commands us not to be drunk with wine also commands us with the same authority to be filled with the Holy Spirit.

We may escape the sin of commission and be guilty of the sin of omission. It is possible to fail in God's work and still be a teetotaller. Do you not think it is a greater sin to fail to do what we ought to do than to do what we ought not to do? If we do what we ought to do we will not be what we ought not be.

Obedience to this command to "Be filled with the Spirit" demands the following:

A complete commitment to the Holy Spirit. To be filled by the Holy Spirit is equal to being under the control of the Holy Spirit. For me to be filled with the Spirit means handing over the key to my life and will to God for His total control. Just as a drunk man is under the control of alcoholic spirits so the Spirit-filled man is under the control of God.

The continual control of the Holy Spirit. Paul's command, "Be filled with the Spirit," does not imply a one-off experience. The command suggests, "Keep on being filled with the Holy Spirit." It is meant to be a continuous and ongoing experience for the Christian.

The Apostles were baptized by the Holy Spirit at Pentecost. Luke never records again in Acts that they were baptized, on another occasion but they were repeatedly filled by the Holy Spirit many times. As Christians we need to know the inflow of God filling our lives every day. A drunk man becomes drunk by drinking. He continues to stay drunk by continuing to drink. Likewise the Christian needs to enjoy the continual supply of the Holy Spirit in his life.

The conscious claiming of the Holy Spirit. As Christians we need to be aware that all that we need we already have. Often we tend to cherry-pick and ask God for qualities such as more patience or more power. When we have the Holy Spirit we have the One who is powerful and whose fullness enables us to be patient.

Not too far from our home in County Down, Northern Ireland there are several reservoirs nestled in the Mourne Mountains. With our plentiful rainfall these reservoirs are nearly always full which means we seldom ever lack water to our homes. The reservoir of heaven is full. It is important that heaven's fullness flows to us and through us so that we enjoy the Spirit-filled Christian life.

2. Because of the obligations of my walk. (Ephesians 5:1,2,8,15)

Without the fullness of the Holy Spirit it is impossible to rightly fulfil the obligations which Paul mentions following his command to be filled with the Holy Spirit.

The obligations of my worship. "Speaking to yourselves in psalms and hymns and spiritual songs, singing and making melody in your heart to the Lord; Giving thanks always for all things unto God and the Father in the name of our Lord Jesus Christ" (5:19,20). The primary result of the Spirit's control in the believer's life is worship to God. The Saviour said, "The hour cometh, and now is, when the true worshippers shall worship the Father in spirit and in truth: for the Father seeketh such to worship him. God is a Spirit: and they that worship him must worship him in spirit and in truth" (John 4:23,24).

The obligations of my wedding. "Submitting yourselves one to another in the fear of God. Wives, submit yourselves unto your own husbands, as unto the Lord. For the husband is the head of the wife, even as Christ is the head of the church: and he is the Saviour of the body. Therefore as the church is subject unto Christ, so let the wives be to their own husbands in every thing. Husbands, love your wives, even as Christ also loved the church, and gave himself for it" (5:21-6:4). Spirit-filled living is most practical. It is not just for worship in the church. When God fills and controls our lives heaven can fill the home.

The obligations of my work. "Servants, be obedient to them that are your masters according to the flesh, with fear and trembling, in singleness of your heart, as unto Christ; Not with eyeservice, as menpleasers; but as the servants of Christ, doing the will of God from the heart; With good will doing service, as to the Lord, and not to men" (6:5-7). It is interesting that Paul addresses the Christian's relationships at work before he came to the matter of spiritual warfare. The effective Christian is one who is filled with the Holy Spirit so that others will see his witness by the work that he does.

The obligations of the warfare. "Finally, my brethren, be strong in the Lord, and in the power of his might. Put on the whole armour of God, that ye may be able to stand against the wiles of the devil" (6:10-18). Spiritual conflict has been the core of our study in this book, but it is interesting that Paul's reference to the Christian's engagement in spiritual warfare flows from his command to filled with the Holy Spirit.

The obligations of my witness. "And for me, that utterance may be given unto me, that I may open my mouth boldly, to make known the mystery of the gospel, For which I am an ambassador in bonds: that therein I may speak boldly, as I ought to speak" (Ephesians 6:19,20). Paul solicited the prayers of the Ephesian for his witness. His request reflects the promise of the Lord Jesus to the Apostles in Acts 1:8; "Ye shall receive power, after that the Holy Ghost is come upon you: and ye shall be witnesses unto me both in Jerusalem, and in all Judaea, and in Samaria, and unto the uttermost part of the earth." The energy and power of the apostolic witness for Jesus Christ was the fullness of the Holy Spirit. How much more do we need the Holy Spirit in our service for Jesus Christ?

3. Because of the opportunities in the world.

The context of Paul's command "Be filled with the Spirit," suggests that the distinctive mark of the Christian life is the fullness of the Holy Spirit. "See then that ye walk circumspectly, not as fools, but as wise, Redeeming the time, because the days are evil. Wherefore be ye not unwise, but understanding what the will of the Lord is. And be not drunk with wine, wherein is excess; but be filled with the Spirit" (5:15-18).

We must spend our time wisely. Any day not crowned by the fullness of the Holy Spirit is a day misspent.

We must spread the truth fully. A hungry and needy world around us needs Spirit-filled Christians.

4.   Because of opposition in the spiritual world

The secret of the life of victory in the spiritual world is to know the fullness of the Holy Spirit. We are up against all the artillery of hell. "We wrestle not against flesh and blood but against principalities, against powers, against the rulers of the darkness of this world, against spiritual wickedness in high places". We cannot overcome by human strength. We are no match for the unholy trinity of the world, the flesh and the devil; however, greater is He who is in us than He who is in the world (1 John 4:4).

Christian friend, God has provided all the energy and equipment we need to be the overcomers the Lord intended us to be. "For whatsoever is born of God overcometh the world: and this is the victory that overcometh the world, even our faith. Who is he that overcometh the world, but he that believeth that Jesus is the Son of God?" (1 John 5:4,5).

Paul declared to the Corinthians, "But thanks be to God, which giveth us the victory through our Lord Jesus Christ" (1 Corinthians 15:57). Again to the Corinthian believers he expressed his confident thanksgiving, "Now thanks be unto God, which always causeth us to triumph in Christ" (2 Corinthians 2:14).

There is no reason to be a defeated Christian. Everything we need to be victorious is provided for us in Jesus Christ. At Calvary Jesus Christ overcame Satan and we can live in the enjoyment of that victory.

In the first three chapters of Revelation the Lord promises, rich rewards to those who will overcome through our Saviour:

"To him that overcometh will I give to eat of the tree of life, which is in the midst of the paradise of God" (Revelation 2:7).

"He that overcometh shall not be hurt of the second death" (Revelation 2:11).

"To him that overcometh will I give to eat of the hidden manna, and will give him a white stone, and in the stone a new name written, which no man knoweth saving he that receiveth it" (Revelation 2:17).

"He that overcometh, and keepeth my works unto the end, to him will I give power over the nations" (Revelation 2:26).

"He that overcometh, the same shall be clothed in white raiment; and I will not blot out his name out of the book of life, but I will confess his name before my Father, and before his angels" (Revelation 3:5).

"Him that overcometh will I make a pillar in the temple of my God, and he shall go no more out: and I will write upon him the name of my God" (Revelation 3:12).

"To him that overcometh will I grant to sit with me in my throne" (Revelation 3:21). Christian, you were born again to be an overcomer. With such great promises from God's Word and the provision made for us in Jesus Christ you need not be overcome by evil. Realise what is yours through the Holy Spirit and be an overcomer through Jesus Christ.

STUDY QUESTIONS

1. List from Ephesians several of the roles the Holy Spirit plays in the life of the Christian.

2. In your opinion what is the difference between the Holy Spirit's residence in the Christian and His filling of the Christian?

3. What does it mean to be filled with the Holy Spirit?

4. What reasons can you give why the Christian should be filled with the Holy Spirit?

5. On what grounds should the Christian be an overcomer instead of being overcome?